JEAN BAUHAUS

Self-Publishing for the Broke Author

How to Edit Your Manuscript, Format Your Book and Create a Killer Cover on Little to No Money

Contents

Introduction

It costs a lot of money to produce a book of high enough quality to have any chance of competing in a saturated publishing market. Between professional editing, formatting and hiring a talented cover designer, you can expect to spend anywhere from hundreds to thousands of dollars, and if you can't bankroll that yourself, your only hope is to run a successful Kickstarter campaign to cover your production costs.

At least, according to some people.

I recently read an article from a self-published author who spent over ten grand to produce and publish his book. He happened to be well off to begin with, and he could afford to hire the best of the best — editors and cover illustrators who worked for major New York publishing houses and freelanced on the side. Good for him! Trouble was, he was not only advocating that those reading his article spend the same amount of money to publish their own books, but he seemed to assume that this was the only way to self-publish and have any hope of success.

I call B.S.

Who am I, and why does my opinion matter?

I'm an author of about ten books (and counting), most of which are fiction, many of which are self-published. My first experiment in self-publishing was my debut novel, which was released in 2011. This is how much I spent to produce that novel: Zero dollars.

I accomplished this by doing everything myself, with the help of well-read and eagle-eyed friends who served as beta readers and proofreaders. To be fair to Mr. Ten Grand, I had a background in both graphic design and copy editing, so I had the skills to produce a solidly professional-looking book. It was a lot of work, and took a lot of my time, but it paid off. While it wasn't a runaway bestseller, that novel gained me a small but devoted following who has snapped up every book I've published since. Better yet, eventually that self-published novel landed me a three-book contract with a mid-sized traditional publisher to turn it into a series, leading to my current status as a hybrid author — one who is both traditionally published and self-published.

My second self-published novel, released the following year, cost me around $50. That was the combined cost of the stock photos I wanted to use on the cover. I was still broke at the time, so I ran an Indiegogo campaign to pre-sell copies to my small but devoted handful of followers to cover the costs. That book was also not a bestseller, but it's performed respectably enough, gaining me another small but devoted set of fans and generating a lot of positive reviews.

Since then I've self-published several more novellas and short stories, and now that I've fulfilled my traditional publishing contract, I'm ready to return to self-publishing. I'm curently in the process of preparing the sequel to my second self-pubbed novel. I've also parlayed the skills and knowledge I picked up by producing those books into a side business, editing and formatting books and coaching authors through the self-publishing process.

This is my first non-fiction book — also self-published. I wrote it because I don't want the voices telling you that self-publishing a quality book is prohibitively expensive to be the only voices you hear. I want you to know that it's entirely possible to produce a book of excellent quality at any budget — even no budget at all — if you're willing to put in the necessary time and hard work. And on the following pages, I'm going to tell you how.

And because I don't want you to remain a broke author, I'm also going to guide you through creating an effective platform and employing no-cost marketing tactics to grow your reader base and lay the groundwork for long-term success, all while you write your next book.

This is not a book about how to write best sellers, how to get rich or even make a living writing and publishing, or any of those things, so if you thought that was the sort of book you were getting, you should go ahead and return it for a refund. The point of this book is simply to help you get started with your first book and lay a solid foundation for a long-term writing and publishing career. If that sounds good to you, then let's get started.

How to Use This Book

You can read this book linearly, from beginning to end, or feel free to skip around as needed. And because everybody is different and no solution is one-size-fits-all, you can also feel free to take the advice that works for you, leave what doesn't, and adapt any of it to suit your own needs. You can also flip straight to the back to find a list of free or low-cost tools and resources that will help you along your indie author journey.

At the end of each section, you'll also find questions designed to help you create your own strategy and develop your own path to becoming a self-published author and growing your reader tribe. You can grab a notebook and answer them there, or click here to download a set of free printable worksheets that you can fill out as you go.

Prepare to Achieve Your Dream

Your dream of becoming a published author is well within your grasp. If you have a finished, well-written manuscript, a computer with internet access, determination and a willingness to put in time and hard work, you have everything you need to achieve that dream — no money required. My hope is that everyone reading this book will find the tools you need to not only achieve your dream of holding your own book in your hands and having it read by strangers, but that you will go on to achieve long-term success and enjoy a long and fulfilling writing and publishing career.

Ready to get started? Then roll up your proverbial sleeves, and let's dive in.

I

Producing Your Book

Editing and Proofreading

I can't stress enough how important a good edit is for your book. I tend to raise an eyebrow when I see independent authors publishing a new book every month or so. I can't help but wonder how much time they spent editing those books. And when I bother to read them? Often the answer appears to be, not very much time at all.

Look, I get it. The competitive nature of self-publishing tends to reward those who can crank out the most books in the least amount of time. And a lot of readers, depending on the genre, don't really care how well a book is edited as long as it entertains them or has good info.

But there are also a lot of readers out there who DO care, and who won't hesitate to shred a badly-edited or, worse, completely unedited book in the review section.

I also concede that there are authors out there who can pull off such a fast draft-to-publication turnaround without compromising on editing. Some such authors have a good rapport with their editors and have a carefully-honed and smoothly-oiled system in place for producing books quickly without compromising on quality. And there are some authors who are simply good at producing clean first drafts that don't need that much editing to begin with. I've even managed to be such an author once or twice in my career.

But most of the time, my own manuscripts require two to three times as long to revise and edit as they did to write in the first place, and they are always, ALWAYS better for having gone through the editing process.

If you want to be the kind of author who consistently gets positive reviews and has a devoted readership who is happy to evangelize about your books to others, then don't skip or skimp on the editing process. And if you have any money to spend on book production, this is where I most recommend you spend it.

Does this mean you have to spend money to hire a professional editor? No, it does not. But before I get into the budget-friendly options, let's first talk about the stages and types of editing.

Stages of Revision

Ideally, a manuscript will go through several stages before it's ready to be published. The first, of course, is the drafting stage, wherein the book actually gets written. No duh, right? Let's move on.

The second stage usually encompasses your own revisions. This is the part where you read through what you've written — preferably after you've had enough of a break from looking at it and thinking about it that you're seeing it with at least semi-fresh eyes — and fix the problems that you yourself are capable of spotting and identifying, polishing your prose as you go. By the end of this stage, you'll have what amounts to your second draft. Simple enough.

Now this is where it can tricky. Do you send your second draft to an editor, or do you send it to beta readers first? Or do you show it to a trusted first reader and complete a third draft based on their feedback before showing it to anyone else? Depending on how much time you have and on the budget editing strategy you settle on, there could be any number of additional passes at this stage. Let's say, at a minimum, you want to have beta readers look it over before you send it to an editor.

Why not just send it to the editor first and let them fix everything? Because regardless of whether you are paying cash money for a professional editor's services or you've convinced your high school English teacher to look it over in exchange for helping her grade essays, your editor will be able to do a better job if you have already cleaned up your manuscript as much as possible on your own. Speaking as someone who has done her fair share of freelance editing, I can promise you that an editor is better able to focus on what can improve your story and the overall quality of your prose when she's not bogged down in correcting grammar, punctuation and sentence structure.

Also, contrary to popular belief, it's not actually an editor's job to fix your book. It's an editor's job to point out problems and, when appropriate, offer suggestions. It's still your job to fix said problems. Exactly how much hands-on revising an editor does depends on the type of edit she's been hired to do, which we'll get into in the next section.

But the point is, between the second draft and final pass of your manuscript, you want to have as many eyes that are not yours on your manuscript and gather as much feedback as possible — all of which leads to the final stage: proofreading, which should be the absolutely last pass of your manuscript, after all other revisions have been done. Why? Because every new revision and editing pass creates opportunities to introduce new errors and typos. The final proofreading pass is for the purpose of hunting down and zapping these errors out of existence, as much as humanly possible.

Types of Editing

A lot of writers aren't aware that there are different types of editing, each of which serves a different purpose. Let me break them down for you.

Developmental Editing - Also known as substantive editing, this type of editing is typically done early on. It looks for potential problems with the story itself: pacing, plot holes, inconsistencies, lack of character development, scenes that put the reader to sleep, that sort of thing. A lot of these problems can be identified and worked out with a good team of beta readers; but if you're stuck and feel like you need professional help to get yourself out of a hole, this is a good type of editing to invest in.

This type of edit can range from a critical analysis of your manuscript, in which the editor simply makes suggestions and leaves it up to you to make the changes; to hands-on editing that rips out the parts that aren't working, rearranges scenes or sections for better flow and also offers suggestions that you, the author, can choose to implement. Obviously, the more hands-on an editor is with your book, the more it's going to cost you.

Copy Editing - Also known as line editing, this type of edit looks at the writing: sentence structure, awkward phrasing, grammar and syntax issues, etc. This is probably the most common type of edit that gets hire out to professionals, as it's what most people think of when they think of editing.

If you invest in this type of edit, look for an editor who is willing to provide a sample edit and make sure they will actually improve your writing and not simply stomp all over your voice and style. Ideally, a professional editor will simply point out things that need to be fixed and, although they may offer suggestions, ultimately they'll leave how to fix it up to you.

Proofreading - This type of edit searches your manuscript with a fine tooth comb to spot and correct errors of spelling, typing, punctuation, grammar, syntax, formatting, etc. As mentioned previously, this should be the absolute final edit, and it should be done by someone other than yourself, and it should involve more than simply running spell check.

How much can you expect to pay for these types of edits? It will largely depend on the type of edit you're getting, the size of your manuscript, the quality of your writing to begin with, and the experience and reputation of the editor. In general, for a full-sized novel or non-fiction book, you can expect to spend anywhere from several hundred to several thousand dollars.

Obviously, if you're reading this book, that's very likely an unrealistic proposition.

Before we move on, I should point out that most freelance editors worth their salt will let you pay in installments, and some even offer financing. However, I don't recommend or advocate that you go into debt in order to get your book edited. The sad reality is that, unless lightning strikes and you turn out to be the next E.L. James or Hugh Howey, you won't make your money back — at least not on this one book.

So where does that leave you? Fortunately, with a few options.

Editing on a Budget

Whether you've got a little money to invest in editing, or you're working with no money at all, don't fret. Editing is not an all-or-nothing proposition. You've still got options.

Remember, you can find links to all of the online resources mentioned below at daydreamerpublishing.wordpress.com/brokeauthor/resources.

If You Have a Little Money...

Invest in ProWritingAid, an AI-driven app that bills itself as a "grammar guru, style editor, and writing mentor in one package." While it's always preferable to have actual human eyes check your work, an AI editor might be the next best thing, and this one can do many of the same things an editor could do for you. Premium packages start at $60 per year, which is a fraction of the cost of hiring a person, especially considering you can use it as often as you need (they also have a less robust free version if you're dealing with a no money situation).

Ask for a partial edit. Most freelance editors will be happy to edit a single chapter or even a few pages. Send in the roughest or most problematic section of your manuscript and request a line edit. You can then use that edit as a guide as you self-edit the rest of your book.

Ask for a professional critique, which typically costs substantially less than an edit. If you can afford to send in the entire manuscript, great, but if not, again, most editors will be happy to provide a partial. I've worked with critique clients that have sent me one or two chapters at a time, as they could afford it, which I critiqued and provided feedback as we went.

Give a new editor a chance. Someone who is just starting out and trying to establish an editing business, who doesn't yet have a body of work or experience in this field, will likely charge much less than an established editor. Depending on how eager they are to build their portfolio, they might even be willing to work for free in exchange for referring their services to other writers in your network—but you shouldn't approach them with this expectation. At the very least, offer to pay what you can.

Try Fiverr.com. Fiverr is a freelance marketplace that got its name from the initial idea that freelancers would provide their services starting at only five dollars. The site has grown up quite a bit since then, and while you can expect most service providers to charge substantially more than a fiver for their work, you can find a wide range of services and experience levels that make it fairly easy to find editing and other publishing-related services that fit your budget (side note: if you have some kind of service to offer, Fiverr could also be a good way to start your own side business that will help pay for your editing).

Save your money for the proofreader. If you feel confident that you're able to work out story issues with the help of trusted beta readers and polish your prose to a level that leaves both you and your readers satisfied, then you're better off hiring a proofreader anyway. And proofreading typically costs quite a bit less than substantive or line editing.

If You Have No Money...

Join a writing or critique group. Whether you meet with one in person or online, a writing group can provide valuable feedback on your manuscript. While it won't cost you any money, it will cost quite a bit in time, as you'll be obligated to return the favor by reading and providing feedback on the other members' work.

Assemble a team of trusted beta readers. Look for people who not only have a good grasp of grammar and sentence structure, but who are well-read and familiar with the genre in which you're writing. Be sure to recognize that they're giving up their valuable time to do you a favor, even if they seem excited to read your book. Provide them with deadlines, but don't hound them or guilt them if they're not able to deliver. And be sure to compensate them in some way, whether that's thanking them by name in the book's acknowledgments, providing them with free copies of the final book, or baking them cookies to show your appreciation. For more information on working with beta readers to edit your book, head to daydreamerpublishing.wordpress.com/brokeauthor/resources and download my free booklet, Seven Steps to Self-Editing for Indie Authors on a Shoestring.

Barter or trade for editing services. Do you have editing skills and know another writer who does editing on the side (or vice versa)? Offer to swap manuscripts—you'll edit hers if she'll edit yours. Editing isn't the only thing you can trade. Can you help a freelance editor improve her website or beef up her SEO? Can you write some articles for her blog? Is there someone local to you for whom you could provide a more hands-on service such as yard work, house cleaning or babysitting? See also my previous example of helping your old English teacher grade papers. Get creative. There are a lot of different ways to "pay" for editing services that don't involve money.

Use Grammarly.com, a free online app that can check your writing for spelling and grammar errors, passive voice and misused words as you go. There's also the free version of ProWritingAid that I mentioned above.

As you can see, not having a budget set aside for hiring an editor is not the end of the world, nor is it the end of your self-publishing ambitions. With a combination of creativity, time and sweat equity, there are plenty of other paths you can take to achieve a polished, publishable book.

Your Strategy

Take time to answer the questions at the end of each chapter to help you develop your budget publishing strategy.

1. What my manuscript needs the most help with is:

2. Who do I know who would make a good beta reader?

3. For each person listed above, list their strengths (I.e., good grasp of grammar, eagle-eyed typo spotter, good understanding of story structure, pacing, etc., good knowledge of my genre).

4. How much money, if any, could I allocate to editing?

5. Which type of edit would give me the most bang for my buck?

6. Who in my network has editing skills and might be willing to barter with me?

7. What skills or abilities do I have to barter with?

Formatting and Book Design

Confession: I started another version of this book several years ago, before my novel-writing career took an unexpected turn and I got sidetracked with a traditional publishing contract. Back then, I had an entire chapter devoted to do-it-yourself e-book formatting. It's probably a good thing this book got delayed for so long, because in the intervening years, the available free tools for creating a professionally laid out e-book have come a long, long way, making it unnecessary to hire a professional formatter in the majority of cases.

When would you need to consider bringing in a professional? For graphic-heavy books or books with specialized layouts—textbooks, photography-heavy cook books or coffee table books, graphic novels, illustrated children's books and the like. In these cases, it's not simply a matter of knowledge and skill, but also of possessing the correct (often expensive) software and knowing how to use it, which is where a well-equipped professional can really come in handy. For budget-friendly help with formatting those kinds of books, I would once again recommend checking out Fiverr.com, where you stand a good chance of finding affordable professional assistance.

But for most novels and straightforward, text-based non-fiction, the following options should meet all your formatting needs.

E-book Formatting

E-books come in two flavors: Mobi, which is Amazon's proprietary e-book format and is what you're looking at any time you read a book on a Kindle device or app; and Epub, which is the file format that works with the Nook, Kobo Reader, and pretty much every other non-Kindle device. If you're going to publish exclusively on Amazon — say, if you decide to enroll in their Kindle Select program so that your books will be available in Prime Lending and Kindle Unlimited — then you only need to worry about creating a Mobi version of your book. If you're planning on a wider distribution, then you'll also need an Epub version. If that sounds complicated, don't worry. All of the methods mentioned below are capable of producing both.

If You Have a Little Money...

If you can afford it, I recommend investing in a good piece of software like Scrivener, which is what I typically use to create all of my e-books, including this one. If you're using a Mac, I've also heard excellent things about a formatting program called Vellum, which has a reputation for both being user-friendly and producing gorgeous book layouts. It carries a hefty price tag, however, and again, it's only available for Mac users.

Scrivener is not only much more affordable, it's also available for both Mac and Windows. It's primarily a writing program, and while it has a bit of a learning curve to use (although there is no lack of tutorials to be found with a quick Google search), I love it for outlining and organizing my manuscripts. Since I use Scrivener to write my books anyway, once my manuscripts are ready to publish, I use the built-in e-book creation tool to create my Mobi and Epub files. They look more utilitarian than what you can get with Vellum, but with some creative tweaking it is possible to add some creative design flourishes to e-books produced with Scrivener.

If You Have No Money...

MS Word + Calibre - While Word is by no means a free or inexpensive program, I mention it only because so many people either already have it on their computers or have access to it on their work computers (if you don't, then you can download Open Office Writer, a free open source Word knock-off that has many of the same capabilities). Calibre is a free e-book management program you can download that will allow you to convert your Word (or Open Office) files to .epub or .mobi. And if you know a little about coding HTML and CSS and like to have hands-on control of how your book will look, Calibre will also let you go in to your e-book files and tweak your book's appearance.

Smashwords' Meat Grinder - While this will only work for books you plan to sell and distribute through Smashwords.com, if you already have Word or Open Office and you're not so particular about the output as long as it's readable, you can simply upload your .doc to their website and let their "Meat Grinder" do all of the work of creating all of the different e-book files you could ever want. Just be aware that they have exacting formatting standards that your document must meet in order for their program to work properly, all of which are detailed in the free *Smashwords Style Guide.*

Draft2Digital.com - Along with Smashwords, I'll discuss this service in more detail once we get to the Publishing section, but for now it's worth mentioning that if you use this service to distribute your book, they also have decent built-in conversion software that can turn your Word doc into the appropriate e-book files.

Reedsy Book Editor - Reedsy.com offers both an online marketplace to connect indie authors with freelance publishing professionals, and free tools and resources to help you along in your self-publishing journey. One of those free tools is the Book Editor, an online book formatting and typesetting app capable of producing both e-books and paperback interior layouts. I recently used this tool to format a short story collection, and while the results weren't perfect — I had to try a couple of different templates before I found one that didn't render my e-book entirely in italics, and the paperback version printed the chapter title in the running header where I would have preferred to have my author name instead — overall, I was impressed. It was easy to use and the resulting books looked very professional.

As you can see, there is no shortage of free options available, all of them capable of producing perfectly presentable e-book files. If you're only planning to publish e-books, you can skip to the strategy questions at the end of the chapter. Otherwise, keep reading to learn about your budget-friendly options for creating paperback interiors.

Paperback Interiors

Where e-book creation is fairly simple, paperbacks can get a little trickier to do on your own. For this reason, many indie authors decide to skip offering paperbacks or hard copies altogether and stick to e-books.

While that's a valid strategy that has worked just fine for many self-published authors, there are a few good reasons to consider putting together a paperback, such as…

- If you don't offer a paperback, you're leaving out potential readers and fans who either don't have a way to read e-books or who simply hate e-books on principle.

- If you ever hope to sell your books at conventions or do book signings, you'll need a stack of paperbacks to sell.

- Contrary to popular belief, it is possible to get self-published paperbacks into brick-and-mortar bookstores and libraries.

- On your Amazon e-book's page, your e-book's price will display as a markdown from your paperback's price, making book shoppers think they're getting a bargain when they buy your e-book. This reason alone is why I usually offer a paperback even though they don't sell nearly as well as my e-books.

Make no mistake, though: paperback formatting can be a painstaking process. And again, if you're doing a book with a specialized layout and/or a lot of graphics, then unless you're a formatting expert, it's time to bring in a pro. Only you can decide whether the above reasons are worth the hassle. If you believe they are, then read on.

The Process of Paperback Book Production

Despite how I made it sound above, the process of creating a paperback is actually pretty straightforward. You simply format your manuscript according to your chosen trim size and the printer's (in this case, the POD publisher of your choice) specifications, which is something that can be accomplished in Word or OpenOffice. You then export the file as a PDF with embedded fonts, and upload that file to your publishing platform, along with your cover image file. Simple, right?

Simple, but that's not the same thing as easy. In newer versions of Word, the process is pretty straightforward, although if you're adding images, that can make things a bit tricky. And creating section breaks and properly formatted running headers in older versions of Word or in Open Office tends to be even more of a battle. For that reason, DIY formatting is not something I recommend that you attempt from scratch. But never fear. Whether you have a little money or no money to work with, you've got options.

You can find links to all of the apps and resources mentioned below at daydreamerpublishing.wordpress.com/brokeauthor/resources.

If You Have a Little Money...

Invest in good formatting software. As mentioned in the previous chapter, for Mac users, Vellum is the go-to software for e-book formatting, and they offer a full package that includes paperback formatting for an additional $50 over their base price. It's pricey software, and again, it's only available for Mac. But if you can swing it, it would be a valuable tool for all of your future books.

Purchase a pre-made template. Beautiful pre-formatted templates created to work with MS Word or Apple's Pages are plentiful, and typically carry an affordable price tag. If you're using Open Office, you should be able to use a Word template, although it may require a bit of finagling to work properly. You can find these easily with a Google search, but I'll include links to my favorites in the back of this book.

If You Have No Money...

Download a free MS Word template from Kindle Direct Publishing. It won't be fancy, but it will take a lot of the guesswork out of setting the correct margins, section breaks, headers and justification, and save you a lot of time spent fiddling around with the settings.

Try Reedsy Book Editor. As mentioned in the previous section on e-books, the PDF that was produced using this app at Reedsy.com didn't meet my exacting standards one hundred percent, but it came very close, and what it didn't get right was far from being a deal breaker. Considering that it took a fraction of the time that I usually spend formatting paperbacks in Word, this might become my new go-to method of creating paperback interiors.

Let KDP or Draft2Digital create a paperback from your e-book file. Once again, this is not something I've tried myself. But it is an available option, and it's free, which makes it worth mentioning.

Once your book files are properly formatted for e-book and paperback, you're well on your way to being ready to publish. There's just one more missing piece. We'll look at your book cover options in the next chapter.

Your Strategy

Take time to answer the questions at the end of each chapter to help you develop your budget publishing strategy.

1. How much money, if any, can I afford to invest in professional formatting, formatting software or professional templates?

2. What software or apps are already available to me?

3. If I can invest in only one type of formatting, e-book or paperback, which am I most comfortable doing myself?

4. Do I want to include a paperback book, or only publish an e-book? What's my reasoning for this?

5. Is there anyone in my network with whom I might be able to trade or barter for formatting services, or who might be willing and able to help me? If so, list them here.

6. What would I be able to offer them in return?

23

Cover Design

Your book's cover is probably the single-most important element of your book — yes, even more important than editing. Why? Because while shoddy editing might earn you some bad reviews, a shoddy cover can tank your sales from the very beginning. A great cover, on the other hand, can practically sell your book for you.

If you have some money and can only spend it on one aspect of book production, this is where you should spend it. And if you don't have money, you can try the same bartering tactics described in the previous chapter. But if you're stuck designing your own cover and you don't know Photoshop from Illustrator or a brush from a vector, don't panic. That doesn't mean your book is automatically doomed to have a terrible cover. You've still got some pretty great options. To find out what they are, keep reading.

Creating Your Cover

Before we explore your options, there are a few things you need to know. For one thing, if you've decided to publish a paperback as well as an e-book, then you're going to need two versions of your cover. In this case, it's best to design your paperback cover first, and then convert the front cover into your e-book cover.

If you did this in reverse order, you'd run into a couple of problems. First, your paperback cover wouldn't be the proper resolution for print. Second, you might have text and other important elements fall outside the designated print area, which means they would appear out of place or cut off on the printed version of your book.

For a paperback cover, you need to decide whether to do full wraparound cover design that includes the back cover and spine. This depends largely on which POD publisher you're planning to use. I'll discuss each of these POD publisher's pros and cons in the next chapter, but here's what you need to know for now: IngramSpark will require you to provide a wraparound cover for paperbacks, and they also allow you to print hardcovers, which opens up an entirely new area of cover requirements. Kindle Direct Publishing's print publishing service (formerly Createspace) will allow you to dispense with a wraparound cover file. Instead, you can simply use their Cover Creator to insert your front cover image into one of their pre-made cover templates. Not only does this make a DIY cover much easier, but also, even if you hire someone, you'll save money by only doing a front cover.

It's also important to get the resolution right. For print book covers, your images will need to be high resolution. That means they need to be rendered at a minimum of 300 pixels per inch (ppi) or dots per inch (dpi). Ebook covers should be standard web resolution, which is 72 ppi/dpi; otherwise, the data size of your image files will be too large and they'll be rejected by the publishing platform.

You can find links to more in-depth information on cover specifications at daydreamerpublishing.wordpress.com/brokeauthor/resources. For now, this information should help you build your cover design strategy.

If You Have a Little Money...

If you can swing it, hire a pro. You can find a good cover designer starting around $250 to $300. Shop around. A good place to start looking is the monthly cover design awards at The Book Designer blog at thebookdesigner.com. Not only can you scope out the work of various freelance cover designers, but you can also read professional critiques of their work and learn what makes a good cover.

If you're willing to take a chance on someone less experienced, or if you're willing to deal with a bit of hassle (i.e. language barrier, vastly different time zones, etc.) to work with someone based overseas, head to Fiverr.com to look for designers who are willing to work for less. You might need to sift through a few (or a few dozen) seller profiles to find the good stuff, but you can find amazing talent there for surprisingly little money. To save you some of the headache of digging, I've rounded up a short list of talented designers selling services on Fiverr, which you can find at the afore-mentioned Broke Author Resources page at Daydreamer Publishing's website.

Buy a pre-made book cover. Many professional cover designers offer a selection of pre-made covers that they will personalize with your title and author name and sell you for a reasonable fee, usually starting around $50. It can be a challenge to find a pre-made cover that's a good fit for your particular book, but if you strike gold, this can be a great way to get a beautiful professional cover for your book.

If You Have No Money...

Use Canva.com, a free online graphic design app, to create your e-book cover. Canva offers a rich selection of beautiful, customizable e-book cover templates for just about every genre that you can tweak to your liking. While I usually design my own covers using Photoshop, this book's cover was designed in Canva. Whether you're writing fiction or non-fiction, this app can help you design a great cover at no cost.

Design your own cover in Gimp, a free, open source image editing program that is very much like Photoshop, which you can find at gimp.org. This software has a learning curve, but you can find dozens of online tutorials to help you learn not only how to use it, but specifically how to use it to design your book cover images.

Canva + Gimp + Cover Creator - As mentioned above, for paperbacks you can use KDP's free Cover Creator to create a back cover and spine from a template that will work with your front cover image. Here's how you can combine these tools to create a beautiful paperback cover:

1. Design your cover in Canva, being sure to leave plenty of margin around your title and author name so that they won't get cut off by the printer. Download your cover image as a print-quality PDF.

2. Import your PDF into Gimp, being sure to set the resolution

to 300 in the dialogue box that pops up after you click on the file. Under Image/Print Size, re-size the image to the correct dimensions to fit the trim size of your book, and then export the file as a PDF. Head to the Broke Author Resources page to find a link for a step-by-step tutorial on exactly how to do this.

3. In Cover Creator, choose one of the templates that lets you insert your own front cover, and upload your PDF.

This method may require some trial and error when it comes to getting your important cover elements inside the print area, but unless you happen to be a graphic designer, this is the easiest no-cost method for creating a professional-quality paperback cover.

Use free graphics in your cover designs. I've included a list of good free image and photo libraries in the back of the book. Canva has its own collection of free images to choose from, but you can also upload your own images or those you downloaded from another source. Just be sure to check the free license on each image to make sure it's licensed for commercial use.

You might find that you have to make some compromises. If you do, I recommend sacrificing a full wraparound cover for the time being, or waiting until you've got more cash flow to publish a paperback and only doing an e-book to start out. One of the wonderful benefits of self-publishing is that there is no limit to how many updates and iterations of your book you can produce, and there is no rule saying that your paperback has to come out at the same time as your e-book. In fact, waiting to launch your paperback until after your e-book has started gaining traction can be a great strategy for drawing more attention to your book and introducing it to an entirely new set of readers. So if you can only afford an e-book cover for the time being, that's not the end of the world—that's actually a clever marketing strategy.

If you decide to design and create your own cover, then I definitely recommend checking out The Book Designer for plenty of free advice on what to do and what not to do when it comes to designing a cover that will help and not hinder your book sales.

Either way, whether you pay for your cover with cash money, sweat equity or a combination of both, your book can boast a fantastic cover that won't break your book sales without breaking the bank.

Your Strategy

Take time to answer the questions at the end of each chapter to help you develop your budget publishing strategy.

1. How much money, if any, can I afford to invest in professional cover design?

2. Based on the above, which option(s) best fit my budget?

_ A professional freelance designer

_ Hiring a designer on Fiverr

_ Purchasing a pre-made cover

_ Designing my own cover

3. Do I know any graphic designers who might be willing to barter their services?

4. If so, what could I offer them in return?

5. How comfortable am I with the idea of creating my own cover?

6. How comfortable am I with learning how to use Gimp?

31

7. Do I need a paperback cover at this time? If so, do I need a
    full wraparound cover?

II

Publishing Your Book

Publishing Platforms

Whether or not publishing your book involves any upfront costs depends entirely on your goals. If you simply want to get a book online and start selling it, you won't need to pay anything up front at all, provided you choose the right options. In most cases, all fees are taken out of your book's sale price each time you make a sale. The remaining amount that you receive is your book royalty.

However, if you have ambitions of getting your book into brick-and-mortar bookstores, or of starting your own publishing imprint and having it listed as the publisher, you will need to shell out some money up front. This will go toward purchasing your own ISBN numbers and toward setup fees with your paperback printer and distributor. I'll go into more detail on these later. For now, it's a good idea to think about your goals as you read through your options.

Publishing Your Ebook

E-book publishing has never been easier. That's great news. The even better news is that you can publish your e-book absolutely free. Here's a quick look at what's involved in publishing an e-book.

The first step, especially if you haven't published before, is to create a publisher account with your publishing platform. This typically involves not only filling out your personal and business information, including your legal name, but also your financial and tax information. Depending on the publisher, you'll either need to provide an e-mail address connected to a Paypal account where you can receive royalty payments, or you'll be asked to provide your checking account number and routing number so you can receive electronic deposits to your bank account. You'll also need to fill out a W-9 with your social security number or employee identification number. If you're not a United States citizen, you'll need to fill out the equivalent form for foreign vendors. The purpose of these forms is so that the publisher can report your taxable earnings, and you won't be allowed to publish your book without first completing this step.

The next step is where it starts to get fun. I think so, anyway. In this step, you create your book's listing. Usually, this first involves filling out all of the meta data for your book: Title, subtitle if applicable, author name, whether it's part of a series, the book's genre category (depending on where you publish, you can place it in anywhere from two to five), and the book's description that will appear on it's listing page and in book catalogs.

You'll also be asked to select key words and phrases for your book. This is an important consideration, and not one to skip or take lightly. The right key words can vastly increase your book's visibility, and also get it placed in additional genre categories, particularly on Amazon. Anything that can help get your book in front of more people is worth giving careful thought and attention. The Creative Penn has an excellent post explaining more about how to choose the right key words, and why it matters. You can find the link to that post at daydreamerpublishing.wordpress.com/brokeauthor/resources.

Once that's done, it will be time to upload your e-book file (your Mobi file at Kindle Direct Publishing, your Epub everywhere else—unless you're having them convert your Word doc as discussed in Chapter Two) and your e-book cover image file. This part can take a few minutes. Even if the upload goes quickly, your files will be run through quality checks to make sure they meet all of the required specifications.

With your files uploaded and accepted, you'll be given a chance to preview your e-book. Don't skip this step, even if you already previewed it on your own e-reading device, and especially if you had your e-book converted from a Word doc. This is your last chance to catch any major errors before your book baby is born into the world. Granted, the beauty of self-publishing is that you can correct errors and republish at any time, but it can be embarrassing to only catch major errors after your book has been purchased and read—especially if the only reason you're finding out about an error is that it's mentioned in a review.

The last step is setting your price and choosing your royalty amount. On Kindle Direct, you'll have the option of choosing a 70 percent royalty if you price your book between $2.99 and $9.99. If your price falls outside of that range, you'll automatically receive a 35 percent royalty on each domestic sale in the U.S. (in either case, international sales royalties will be automatically calculated).

Finally, it's time to hit publish. This entire process typically takes about fifteen minutes, provided you don't run into any errors that you'll need to deal with. Once you've pulled the trigger, it can take anywhere from a few hours to a couple of days for the book to appear online. If it takes more than 48 hours, you should contact customer support.

The processes might have some minor differences depending

on where you're publishing, but generally, this is pretty much what you'll experience across the board. With that said, here are your e-book publishing options.

E-book Publishing Platforms

You could set up publishing accounts and publish individually to each of the major e-book retail outlets, including the giants Amazon, Barnes and Noble, Kobo and iTunes, as well as various smaller venues. But that route is tedious and time-consuming, and you might miss out on some less well-known marketplaces. To get your e-book distributed as widely as possible, I recommend publishing it at all three of the following:

Kindle Direct Publishing - Located at kdp.amazon.com, this is Amazon's publishing platform, and until recently it was the only way to get your books on Amazon. It recently became possible to publish to KDP via Draft2Digital (see below), but as you'll see, D2D takes out their small cut on top of each retailer's cut of your book sales, so the only way to get every penny of that sweet 70 percent Kindle book royalty is to publish directly to KDP. This will also give you tighter control of those all-important categories and key words that can help to make or break your book's visibility and sales.

When you publish on KDP, you'll see an option to enroll your book in Kindle Select. Joining this program will get your book into Kindle Unlimited and the Prime Lending Library, and for each borrow you'll receive as payment a portion of the global fund, which is essentially a big pot of money that Amazon splits among the borrowed books in this program, paid out on each book according to the number of pages read.

Another benefit of joining Select for 90 days—the length of the enrollment period, at the end of which you can decide whether to opt out or re-enroll for another 90 days—is that you're given the ability to run promotional sales or limited-time free runs to help gain exposure and reviews.

The drawback of joining this program is that it requires your e-book to be sold exclusively on Amazon during the enrollment period. You can have a paperback for sale on Amazon and other retailers, but your e-book can't be sold, published or posted anywhere else—not even on your own website. This is a pretty major drawback. Many authors make a decent living publishing exclusively on Amazon and reaping the rewards of book borrows, and the Select program has been a great way to grow your audience—as long as you don't mind leaving out potential readers who have non-Kindle devices or prefer not to shop on Amazon.

Another important thing to consider regarding Select is that, as of this writing, many authors and publishers have been reporting declining sales on Amazon. Historically, sales on Amazon have tended to be stronger than on other e-book retailer sites, primarily because Amazon's search and recommendation algorithms made book discoverability easy.

But that appears to no longer be the case. It seems that Amazon might be moving toward a pay-to-play model for book discoverability, meaning that if you want Amazon users to be able to organically discover your book, you'll have to pay for advertising and promotion—much the same way Facebook started limiting who sees posts from pages when they rolled out their paid post promotion program. This is a good example of why it's not a good idea to put all of your eggs in one basket, especially when you don't own that basket. You never know when it might spring a leak, or whether the bottom might fall out completely.

Draft2Digital.com - While D2D is not itself a retailer, this service will distribute your book to all of the major and minor e-book retailers, both domestically and internationally, and also make it available to libraries through Overdrive and Bibliotheca. Recently, they also partnered with Kobo to start making e-books available on Walmart.com, which is a pretty huge deal!

D2D can also distribute your book to Amazon, but as mentioned above, while D2D doesn't charge anything upfront for their services, they take a 10 percent cut from each book sold that was distributed through them, so that would eat into your Amazon profits. It will eat into your profits from other retailers as well, but D2D makes both publishing to those venues and tracking your sales so simple that it's worth losing a few cents on each sale. Also, if you don't have access to a Mac, this is one of the only ways to get your book listed on iTunes.

Smashwords.com - Smashwords is both an e-book retailer and a distributor. Their distribution service is free and includes more or less all of the same retailers as Draft2Digital, plus some additional library distributors. One reason publishing to Smashwords is a must is that they make it possible to generate coupon codes for each of your books, making it easy to run your own book sales on their site, or to give free copies of your book to reviewers. And all without forcing you to publish with them exclusively.

It might seem redundant to publish through both D2D and Smashwords, and you might be wondering right now why you shouldn't skip D2D altogether, especially if they keep 10 percent of your royalties. But there is enough variation in their distribution channels—for instance, Smashwords won't get you into Walmart—that it's best to publish to both in order to reach the widest possible distribution. Also, as you'll see when we get to the section on publicizing your book, D2D offers some powerful book marketing tools that you won't want to do without.

Publishing Your Physical Book

In the early days of print-on-demand publishing, there were quite a few different POD publishers to choose from, all of which provided reasonable quality. Alas, since then the majority of them have been bought out by a scammy company which shall remain nameless (in case you're wondering, it rhymes with Smauthor Polutions) and turned those other publishers into predatory companies that produce shoddy work, making them not even worth mentioning here.

Today, there are basically two worthwhile options for printing your self-published paperback: Kindle Direct Publishing's new paperback publishing service (formerly Createspace) and IngramSpark, the self-publishing arm of the well-known bulk book printer Lightning Source. Each of these has their pros and cons, which I'll discuss below.

Kindle Direct Publishing

As of this writing, I've used Createspace, which is in the process of being phased out and absorbed into KDP, to publish all my paperbacks. My overall experience has been positive, and KDP promises that the things I like about the service won't change.

Whether the cons listed below are actually an issue depends on your goals and ambitions. For many people reading this book, they simply won't matter.

Pros:

- You pay nothing out of pocket. They get paid by keeping the wholesale cost of each book sold and printed to cover production costs. Your royalty depends on how much you mark the price up above wholesale.
- You can publish your Kindle e-book and your paperback on the same account, which is pretty convenient.
- They provide you with a free ISBN number (more on ISBNs in the next section).
- They produce decent-quality paperbacks, and their customer service department is responsive when the occasional printer errors do occur.
- Their publishing interface is streamlined and easy to use.
- Among a number of other helpful free tools and templates, they provide a built-in Cover Creator, making it easy to create your own book cover.
- They offer a wide range of distribution channels, including making your paperback available to brick-and-mortar bookstores, libraries and universities.

Cons:

- You can only print trade paperbacks. They don't offer mass market paperback trim sizes (the size you usually find in supermarket checkout stands), nor do they offer the ability to print hardbacks.

- If you use the free ISBN, Amazon will be listed as the publisher, making it next-to-impossible to convince brick-and-mortar stores to stock your book.
- Even if you supply your own ISBN, with yourself registered as the publisher, it can still be a hard sell getting your KDP book into physical stores, thanks to the fact that KDP doesn't allow bulk wholesale discounts or returns on unsold books. Also, other bookstores just flat out hate Amazon.

IngramSpark

I have not personally used this service, but I've heard great things about it. My understanding is that it's the best way to go if you're determined to get your book into physical bookstores, and it's pretty much your only option if you want to hold a hardback copy of your own book in your hands.

Pros:
- In addition to hardbacks — with or without a dust cover jacket — IngramSpark also offers a wider range of binding options and trim sizes, including mass market paperback sizes.
- They allow bulk wholesale discounts, making books printed with IngramSpark easier to get into brick-and-mortar bookstores.

Cons:

- They charge a $50 setup fee for each print book title, on top of the wholesale production cost they keep from each book printed and sold.
- They also require you to supply your own ISBN. As of this writing, the cost of a single ISBN number is $125. This means that it's going to cost you at least $175 up front in order to publish your book through IngramSpark.
- Additionally, you'll have to supply a full wrap-around cover that includes the back and spine. You can't publish on IngramSpark if all you have is a front cover.

While IngramSpark offers some attractive options, the upfront fees and the additional costs involved in having to provide a wraparound cover — assuming you don't create your own — are going to be a deal-breaker for most bootstrapping authors on a tight budget.

The Brick-and-Mortar Dream

Is getting your book into physical bookstores even a viable possibility at this point, even if you shell out the upfront costs to publish with IngramSpark?

Let's be real for a minute. While I don't want to shoot down your dream, and I don't want to say it's impossible, if you're an unknown, unproven self-published author, it's not very likely. If this is your dream, then this is yet another reason to hold off on publishing a paperback until your e-book has had time to gain traction — not to mention enough royalties to cover the upfront costs involved with IngramSpark.

But you should also be aware that getting your book into physical bookstores is not simply a matter of making it available. It requires a lot of work on your part, calling bookstores and convincing them to carry your book. The more online sales you have, the more attractive your pitch will be to acquisition managers. Nobody wants to buy a book that's likely to just take up space on the shelves and not sell — and if this happens, they'll not only return every copy they bought of your book, but they also won't be likely to take a chance on any of your future titles.

Is it really impossible to get a book printed through KDP into physical stores? Not entirely, but it does require a lot of extra work. Basically, you would have to create your own publishing company, purchase your own ISBN, order a large stock of books that you can then supply directly to bookstores at cost, and have your own system in place for returns.

Of course, all of this changes if your book becomes a major best seller, in which case book stores will be falling over themselves to stock your book, regardless of who is listed as the publisher. But if that happens, then you won't be a broke author anymore, will you?

Publishing Your Audiobook

As with POD publishing, there are really only two viable options for producing and distributing audiobooks, and only one of them offers a method that doesn't require upfront costs—perhaps unsurprisingly, it's the one that's owned by Amazon.

Audiobook Creation Exchange (ACX)

ACX.com is Amazon's audio publishing arm. It exists mainly to help authors self-publish audiobooks to Audible.com.

Pros:

- As the big kid on the block, ACX has a large selection of narrators to choose from.
- A number of those narrators are willing to work for a share of royalties instead of being paid up front.
- More direct contract with your narrator, giving you more control over the final product.
- ACX offers a referral program that will let you earn up to $75 every time a new Audible customer selects your book as their introductory free book—something both you and your narrator can take advantage of to increase your profits.

Cons:

- Exclusivity. If you publish via ACX, your audiobook will only be available on Audible, Amazon and iTunes.
- Anecdotal evidence suggests that as a behemoth that until recently had no competition to speak of, customer service leaves a lot to be desired.

Findaway Voices

The new kid on the block, FindawayVoices.com hopes to give Amazon a run for their money. While there is an initial $49 administration fee if you work with them directly, they have partnered with both Draft2Digital and Smashwords to wave the fee on titles published through either of those services.

Pros:
- No setup fee if you sign up through D2D or Smashwords.
- Wider distribution, including global distribution. Your audio-book will be available pretty much everywhere audiobooks are sold—including Audible.
- A curated selection of narrators to choose from. Some might consider this a con, but if you tend to get overwhelmed by too many choices, this can be a good thing.
- The fact that they're new and eager to prove themselves means they care about customer service.

Cons:
- $49 setup fee if you sign up with them directly.
- You have to hire your narrator and pay them out of your own pocket. Royalty sharing is not an option.
- Less contact with your narrator—basically, beyond getting to sample the first fifteen minutes, you won't know how your book is going until the narrator is done with it.
- No referral program, so you're entirely dependent on book sales and royalties for profit.

While Findaway Voices shows a lot of promise, the out-of-pocket costs involved with hiring a narrator will likely be a deal breaker at this point in your career.

That said, if you're comfortable with doing your own narration, or know someone in your network who could be persuaded to do it for you, that would eliminate the cost of a narrator. You would, however, need to invest in a good microphone and either create or have access to a soundproof area of your home or office (a walk-in closet might do the trick).

You would also have to do your own editing and sound mixing, which you could do using Audacity, a free sound recording and mixing program from SourceForge.net. Editing audio in Audacity is fairly simple, and there are plenty of tutorials to be found online, but be warned that it's a very time-consuming and tedious process—and if you do your own narration, it can be downright painful if the sound of your own voice makes you cringe.

ISBNs and ASINs

With all this talk about ISBNs, you might be wondering what I'm even talking about. ISBN stands for International Standard Book Number, and it's the 10 or 13-digit number you'll find printed on the backs of physical books, as well as on the copyright pages of both print and e-books. On print books, this is also the number encoded in the book's bar code. It helps booksellers track inventory and also provides information such as who the publisher is and helps them look up more information about your book.

In the US, ISBN numbers are sold through Bowker, the one and only official ISBN registrar. There are companies who re-sell ISBNs at a discount, but if you come across such an offer, do your due diligence as a consumer to make sure you don't get ripped off.

You can purchase individual ISBNs at a current rate of $125 each, or you can buy them in bulk, which drives down the per-unit price.

One thing that's important to know about ISBNs is that you can only use a single ISBN number on one iteration of your book. This means that you can't simply buy a single ISBN listing yourself as the publisher and then use that on your e-book, paperback, hardback, audiobook and any other version of the book you produce. You would have to purchase a separate ISBN for each different version. Thank goodness for that bulk discount, right? Even with that going for it, publishing with your own ISBNs tends to be expensive.

Free ISBNs, ASINs and Other Identifiers

The big question is, do you need to buy your own ISBN? As we saw in the last section, the only actual benefit of owning your ISBN listing yourself as the publisher is that it will be easier to get your book into physical bookstores. That's it.

With the exception of IngramSpark, each and every e-book and print publishing platform listed here will supply you with a free ISBN that lists their service as the publisher. And outside of the brick-and-mortar bookstore issue, there is no actual benefit, nor is there any harm, in having your distributor listed as the publisher.

Many online booksellers don't even use ISBNs, and will assign your book a number according to their own internal tracking system. Amazon, for example, assigns each book sold through them an ASIN tracking number. Barnes & Noble and Apple each have their own book ID systems, as well.

So if you're like the majority of indie authors and content to stick to selling your book primarily online, there is no good reason to throw your money away on an ISBN. If you are determined to see your physical book on bookstore shelves, then you still only need to purchase an ISBN for the physical version(s) of your book, as there is absolutely no good reason to buy your own ISBN for your e-book.

My advice for the broke author? Take all the freebies you can get and save your brick-and-mortar ambitions for after you've started to build a name — and an income — for yourself.

Your Strategy

Take time to answer the questions at the end of each chapter to help you develop your budget publishing strategy.

1. What are my long term goals as an author? Take a few minutes to think this out and write them down.

2. How important is it to me to get my book into brick-

and-mortar bookstores at this point in my career? If it is important, WHY does it matter?

3. Can I realistically afford the $125 fee to register my own ISBN? Do I feel like this would be a good investment?

4. Can I afford the $49 setup fee for either IngramSpark or Findaway Voices?

5. Am I able to purchase or create a wraparound cover for my paperback, or will I need to rely on KDP's Cover Creator?

6. Will I be doing appearances or speaking engagements that will require having physical copies of my book for sale?

7. If I answered no above, is it worth it to me to produce either a paperback or an audiobook at this time, or do I want to focus on ebooks for the time being?

8. Do I feel that the benefits provided by the Kindle Select program—enrollment in Kindle Unlimited and Prime Lending, additional promotional tools—are worth remaining exclusive to Amazon for the first 90 days of my book's life?

9. Do I have a way to pay potentially hundreds or thousands of dollars to hire an audiobook narrator?

10. How comfortable am I with the idea of doing my own narration?

11. Do I know anyone who would make a good narrator who might be willing to barter or do me a huge favor?

12. Will I realistically have time to edit my own audio files?

III

Publicizing Your Book

Platform and Author Brand

It's common wisdom that if you want to sell books, you have to have a large platform. This "wisdom"—*it is known, Khaleesi*—ends up getting a lot of new authors stuck in neutral. They write and publish their first book, and then they worry to the point of obsession about building a platform on which to market that one book, and when their website traffic is a slow trickle, their mailing list fails to grow, and their book doesn't sell, they wring their hands in discouragement and then double down on their useless efforts. Some even become so discouraged that they give up and quit writing, or decide that traditional publishing is the only way to succeed as a writer (here's a hint: this stuff isn't any easier for traditionally published authors, and most of them don't have even a fraction of the help with marketing and publicity that you imagine they do).

I was that author. I don't want you to be that author.

I want you to do well, but I want you to understand that self-publishing is about the long game—it's not about overnight success. "Overnight" success almost never comes to people who aren't either already successful, or who haven't spent years toiling in the shadows to lay the groundwork for their success.

If you are reading this book to learn how to publish your first book, you are just getting started. You are beginning to lay that groundwork. And at this point, most marketing you will do is going to be completely pointless until you have a backlog of books.

Not that you shouldn't do any marketing at this stage. There are some bases you should cover, and I'm going to tell you what those bases are and how you should cover them. But I'm here to tell you that once the basics are taken care of, you can go ahead and forget about marketing and write your next book. And the next. And the next, and so on, until you've got enough of a backlog that more advanced marketing and publicity efforts will actually pay off.

Your Author Platform

What is platform? It's everything that you do, both online and off, that will help people find your book. Online, this includes your website, mailing list and social media. It might also include your blog or any other online writing you do, including guest blogging, writing for Medium and/or LinkedIn, etc. It can also include interviews, podcasts or YouTube. Basically, anywhere that you're telling other people that you're an author or that you have a book for sale is part of your platform.

You might already have a solid platform, particularly if your book is non-fiction. Many non-fiction authors already have an established platform before they write their first book. Maybe you have a popular blog or podcast, maybe you have a popular YouTube channel, maybe you get hired for speaking engagements, maybe you do work that places you in the public eye. Maybe that's also true if you're a fiction author. If that's true for you, that's great! You're way ahead of the curve.

The rest of us, though, will be over here building our platforms from the ground up. And that's okay. If you're in this group with us, I'm going to let you in on a little secret: your books are also your platform.

I want you to pause and let that sink in for a minute.

Let me say it again, shout it, even: YOUR BOOKS ARE YOUR PLATFORM!

Each book you write will help publicize your other books. Each book you write will help drive traffic to your website and fill your mailing list with the e-mail addresses of people who can't wait to buy your next book. Each book you write will give you more credibility as an author and make people more curious about what you're writing and what you have to offer them.

So don't get bogged down in marketing. Use that time and energy to write and publish your next book—by doing that, you are actively marketing. You're laying that groundwork. You're not just building a platform, you're building a launchpad, and if you keep at it, sooner or later you're going to skyrocket.

Don't Rush to Publish

I would even suggest that you hold off on publishing your first book until you've at least got a second one written, and possibly even a third. The reality of this business is that once you get your first book out there, you'll be under a lot of pressure to release subsequent books at a quick pace in order to stay competitive—especially if you're writing a series.

This isn't such a big deal if you're a fast writer, but if not, that's all the more reason to hold off. If you're not yet published, then right now you've got all the time in the world to not only write your first two or three books at a pace you're comfortable with, but also to do everything within your budget and ability to produce the best books possible.

Because that's crucial. If this is going to succeed—if your books are going to do a good job of selling both themselves and each other—your books have to be amazing, not only in terms of writing and content, but also in terms of cover design and sales copy (i.e., your book description). So right now, while you can, take the time to get it right.

I don't mean to scare you or trigger your perfectionist tendencies. The good news, and one of the wonderful benefits of self-publishing, is that once your book is out in the world, you can continue to make tweaks and improvements until you get it right. Nothing, not even your title, is set in stone. If a book's not selling as well as you'd like, or at all, you can try a new cover to see if sales pick up. Or you can change your sales copy, or try out a new set of keywords. So that you don't get bogged down in trying to achieve perfection before you pull the trigger on publishing your book, it helps to think of not only each book, but each element of your book, as an experiment—and you can keep experimenting until you find what works.

You simply can't do that in traditional publishing. Once you're book's out there, you're stuck with it as it is.

So take your time, get at least a couple of finished books in your queue so you can release them two or three months apart, and do the best you can with the time and tools you have to make those books the best that they can be, knowing you can always improve them later if you need to. And then go forth and publish, my friend.

What About Brand?

If you listen to marketing experts, you'll also hear a lot about your author brand. Your brand is basically everything you do as an author, and even as a person, both online and offline, that affects how people perceive you and communicates what they can expect, both from you and from your writing. Essentially, you are already a walking, talking author brand, and your books are one element of your brand.

While nailing down your brand is important, I'm going to caution you not to overthink it, especially at this early stage. Your brand will evolve organically as you evolve, and also with each book that you write. It's not about projecting some fake author persona to the world. It's about being your authentic self in a way that will connect with and make you relatable to those who are most likely to enjoy your work. A lot of that will come naturally, and the more you do this, the savvier you'll become. So as you establish the marketing basics we'll cover in the next chapter, give some thought to how it communicates your unique brand, but don't obsess about nailing it on the first try.

For more in-depth explanations of author brand and how to build it (remember: building things takes time!), head to daydreamerpublishing.wordress.com/brokeauthor/resources, where you'll find links to excellent posts on this topic from both The Book Designer and The Creative Penn.

Now let's look at the things you should be doing to lay a solid foundation on which to build up your platform.

Crash Course in Essential Book Marketing

Entire books have been written about book marketing. For that matter, I could tell you enough to fill a book (and I probably will at some point; watch for Book Marketing for the Broke Author, coming soon to a Kindle near you!). Since this is actually a book about publishing, I'm only going to give you the broad strokes in these chapters, just enough to get you started and help you set yourself up right.

The activities I'm going to explain in this chapter are essential. Do not skip them. When combined together, these marketing elements will create a powerful marketing system that will grow your reader tribe and passively market your existing book(s), all while allowing you to keep your head down and focus on writing the next book.

It Starts with Your Books

Like I said in the previous chapter, your books themselves are the most important part of your author platform, and they need to be the best that they can be. That means the content and writing both need to be as excellent as you can make them and they need to be as well-edited and well-formatted as possible.

But even more importantly when it comes to sales, these three elements need to stand out: your title, your cover, and your book's description.

Your Title

If you're writing nonfiction, this is fairly simple—but again, don't confuse simple with easy. The simple part is that there's a formula you can follow: the title grabs the reader's attention; the subtitle explains what the book is about.

Take this book's title: *Self-Publishing for the Broke Author*. It not only says what the book is about, but it also hopefully does so in a catchy way that hooks the reader's attention.

And then the subtitle reels them in with more information: *How to Edit Your Manuscript, Format Your Book and Create a Killer Cover on Little to No Money*.

Taken together, the title doesn't simply tell you what this book is about—it makes a promise about what you can expect that will help the reader determine whether this will be a good investment of their time and money. The subtitle also uses the rule of three: three benefits, described using three action verbs, stated as succinctly as possible.

My original working title for this book was *Indie Publishing on a Budget*. No subtitle. Not only is that somewhat generic and lackluster, it's also way too similar to the title of an already existing book. The other problem is that it doesn't really get to the heart of what this book is about. This isn't a guide to saving money on publishing—it's a guide on how to get it done when you're flat broke. The current title does a much better job of getting that message across.

Let's look at another, more famous and proven, non-fiction title: *Essentialism: The Disciplined Pursuit of Less* by Greg McKeown.

This best-selling title underscores the thesis of the book with a title that is stripped down to the essential elements, and yet it still manages to hook, explain and promise. The rule of threes is also in play, with three key words making up the subtitle.

Coming up with a good title for your fiction can be a lot trickier. There's no real formula to follow, so you've got a lot more room to play, and it's a lot more subjective. The main thing is to make sure it fits the genre in which you're writing, or at least the main genre in which you plan to list your book, if it happens to cross or mash up different genres.

In either case, it pays to research. Whether you're writing fiction or nonfiction, spend some time studying best-selling titles in your genre. Try coming up with a few different titles, and ask your beta readers or people in your network which is most likely to grab their attention and make them take a closer look.

Whatever title you land on, remember that in self-publishing, nothing's written in stone. If something isn't working, you can always come back later and tweak it, or change it altogether. The same is true of your cover and description, too, so while you should do your best on the first try, don't get bogged down in trying to achieve perfection.

Your Cover

Again, when it comes to covers, research is your friend. Study the best-selling covers in your genre, paying close attention to what they each have in common, as well as what they're each doing to stand out. Become well acquainted with TheBookDesigner.com, a blog dedicated to teaching the elements of good cover design as well as layout and typography. Especially helpful are the monthly Book Cover Awards posts, which provide helpful critiques of each entry, explaining what works well and what could be better. Consider submitting your own cover for a chance at a free critique from someone who actually knows what he's talking about.

And while I'm on that subject, it's actually not a good idea to ask your network for opinions on your cover. I've made this mistake a few times myself (it took me a while to learn my lesson) and this can quickly devolve into design by committee, which is an excellent way to ruin your cover. This is one area where you need to learn to trust your gut. And in the same way members of the Secret Service learn how to spot counterfeit money by closely studying the real deal, you need to spend some time training your gut on what a good cover looks like so you'll know if you're not quite there.

To help get you started, here's a quick run-down of what goes into a good book cover:

- It communicates your book's genre.
- It's not cluttered. Pick one or two elements that represent the book. Don't try to cram everything in there.
- Focus on communicating your book's tone, not the plot.
- Choose a font and font color that are easy to read against the background image.
- Choose font sizes that are balanced and still legible when your cover is shrunk down to a tiny thumbnail image.

Kobo Writing Life has a good blog post on what you should focus on in designing your cover, which you can find on the Resources web page.

One more thing: Branding is something you'll want to keep in mind as you design and market each book, particularly if your books are part of a series. As you choose things like your title and the elements of your cover, think about how those can be carried across across multiple books so that your series will have its own cohesive branding that will cue potential readers in that your next book is part of the same series.

Your Book Description

Also known as jacket copy or back cover copy—because these are where the description is typically located on a physical book—your book description has a big job to do. Once your title and cover get your book's proverbial foot in your reader's proverbial door, it's up to your description to deliver your sales pitch.

Once again: Research, research, research. Spend as much time as you can on Amazon or Goodreads, studying the descriptions of best sellers in your genre. Your goal is to hook the reader and give them enough information about your book to intrigue them and make them want to read more without giving the entire plot away.

Here's a simple (but again, not easy) formula for writing your description:

1. Distill your book's plot or message down to one sentence. Make that sentence as punchy as possible. That's your hook, and the first line of your description.
2. Expand that sentence to one or two paragraphs that summarize what your book is about without giving too much away.
3. End with a question that will draw the reader in, or a promise that will entice them to buy.

As an example, here's the current description from my indie novel, Dominion of the Damned:

What if an uncontrollable zombie outbreak took place in a world that contains vampires?

In Dominion of the Damned, the vampires seize their chance to overpower humanity, herd them into labor camps, establish blood mills and prevent the extinction of their only food supply.

Hannah Jordan is a human survivor whose sole mission is to stay alive so she can prevent her orphaned baby brother from becoming monster food.

Aleksandr Konstantin is a vampire whose ideas about how best to preserve humanity are at odds with the established powers that be. He's also a doctor and scientist intent on finding a way to end the zombie threat for good.

When their paths cross, the doctor has a new mission in mind for Hannah-one that he claims could place humanity on equal footing with their vampire overlords. But can she trust him? With her brother's safety at stake, does she really have a choice?

This is probably the third description I've tried for this book, which I'm in the process of re-editing and re-launching in preparation for launching the sequel. It's too soon to tell how well it will work in terms of hooking readers and generating sales, although as of this writing it's starting to gain traction on Wattpad after spending about a month there, so I'm hopeful. The point is this: study, practice, keep tweaking, and if you don't nail it on the first try, try, try again.

Your Sample

If your title and cover are your knock at the door and your description copy is your sales pitch, it's your sample that will seal the deal. Ebook shoppers have the option to download the first ten to fifteen percent of your book, depending on the retailer, to their devices. And on Amazon, they can skip the download and preview your book right there on the listing page via the Look Inside feature.

What does this have to do with you? After all, isn't the amount of the book shown in the preview automatically determined by algorithms or robots or sacrificing a virgin under a blood moon or something like that? Yes (well, probably not the virgin sacrifice part), but: you decide how much of your book's actual content appears in that first ten or fifteen percent, and there's one way to ensure that the preview is almost entirely pure content that is both simple and easy.

Simply move all of the front matter—your copyright page, dedication, etc.—to the back of the book.

A strong word of caution, though: you might have seen this advice before, and it may have also suggested placing your table of contents in the back of the book. While this is not a bad idea on its own merits, do not do this with e-book files you plan to upload to Kindle Direct Publishing. This is against their terms of service, and it could get your booked pulled from Amazon's listings.

Once upon a time, this was a great strategy for providing more real-estate in your book's sample preview for the actual content. Sadly, at some point a few people also realized this was a great strategy for gaming the Kindle Unlimited author payment system, which pays out of the Global Fund for number of pages read. By placing the contents in the back, readers were clicking through to the back of the book without actually reading the book, tricking the algorithms into believing that they had finished reading the book and crediting a full payment to the author. When Amazon got wise to what they were doing, rather than fix the algorithm so that it keeps track of actual pages read, they instead changed their terms of service and started cracking down on books in their system that placed the contents in the back—which at that point was standard practice for self-published e-books, meaning a lot of authors had to scramble to republish their Kindle books with the contents in the front, or else risk having their titles pulled from Amazon's virtual shelves.

Gotta love them bad apples, right?

So anything you publish to Amazon needs to have the table of contents up front. But moving it to the back along with every other page that's extraneous to your book's main event is still a solid strategy for Epub files that you plan to upload anywhere other than Amazon, provided the method you're using to create your Epub allows this option.

Apart from the logistical considerations of where to place your pages to maximize your book sample, you also need to make sure the writing in your sample is your best writing. Once upon a time, your first three chapters needed to be polished to perfection, or as close as you could get to it, because you had three chapters with which to hook an agent or editor and convince them to request the entire manuscript. As far as regular old readers went, you got three pages—the amount the average reader would skim through in a physical bookstore when deciding whether to buy your book.

With attention spans dwindling and e-books allowing readers to make more rapid buying decisions, I think today it's safer to say that you get one page, and probably not even that. More like one paragraph. But that doesn't mean that you should stop polishing your prose to a high sheen after the first paragraph, or even the first page. Your goal is for the reader to be so hooked that they keep reading the sample—and then when they get to the end, they don't hesitate to click *Buy* so they can keep right on reading.

I know it means a lot of work up front, but it's worth taking the time and putting in the effort to get these things right, doing the best you can with the available tools and resources. Because the closer you can get to nailing each of these elements, the harder your book will work to sell itself for you.

Your Website

You need an author website to serve as the main hub of your author platform. That's an actual website, and not just an author page on Amazon or Facebook or Goodreads or About.me or wherever. It's not a bad idea to have those, too, but the only one of these things that is essential is your website, and it should be about you, preferably at yourname.com, and not yourbooktitle.com. Here are just a few reasons why:

- Your website is your space, your little piece of web real estate that you control. You're not limited in what you can post there, you'll never have to worry about having your content suppressed or hidden by algorithms, and it will never shut down unless and until you decide to shut it down.
- A website will help establish your author identity and lend you legitimacy. Any time you reach out to a book blogger,

interviewer or influencer about promoting your book, they'll be able to do a quick search on your name, find your website and see that yes, you are who you say you are, and your book actually exists.

- A website will help build and establish your author brand, and it serves as a main hub where readers, journalists and event organizers can go to find out everything they need to know about you and your books.
- A website is the best place to host a sign-up form for your all-important mailing list, which we'll discuss in the next section.

And here, at a minimum, is what should be on your website:

- A home page displaying your newest and/or upcoming releases and a prominent offer enticing visitors to sign up to your mailing list.
- An about page that includes your author portrait and your author bio—preferably both a short version and a longer version.
- A contact page with all of the best ways to reach you.
- A landing page for each of your books, featuring the cover, the book description, an excerpt, and prominent links to all of the places it can be purchased online.
- A landing page for your mailing list, with a sign-up form or a link to a sign-up page.
- A news and announcements page, or a blog.

Take a look at my fiction author website, JeanMarieBauhaus.com.

It's not fancy, but it gets the job done, and you're welcome to use it as a template.

Should You Have a Blog?

If you enjoy blogging, if you are able to do so consistently, and you have something to write about that isn't boring, go for it. A blog is a great way to incorporate content marketing (more on that in the next chapter) into your website that will pull traffic in from search engines and social media, giving more people more opportunities to sign up to your mailing list and discover your books.

A blog is useless, however, if not done correctly, and it's not essential. If you don't enjoy blogging, or you simply don't have time for it, feel free to skip it and opt for a news and announcements page instead. This will function more or less the same as a blog, but you'll only update it when you have relevant news to share with your readers.

I'll go into more detail in the next chapter about how to get the most out of your blog, if you choose to include one.

Domains and Hosting

Your domain is your web address, or URL. Ideally, your website will live at yourauthorname.com. However, domains do cost money to register each year, and if you're flat broke, then this might have to be a stretch goal for after your books generate some income. They don't cost a lot, though, and if you shop around you can find them very cheaply. My favorite domain host and registrar is Internetbs.net, where you can get your own .com domain for only US$8.49 a year. And if you're able to pay for a hosting plan—even a basic one—typically, a free domain will be included with your plan, so you won't even need to register one separately.

If you haven't already, you're likely to hear at some point that you must have a self-hosted WordPress website. That's WordPress, the free, open source content management system you can download from WordPress.org, not the blogging and website platform at WordPress.com (I know, it's confusing). There are a number of advantages to this, the most-often cited being thus: WordPress hosting is usually cheap—under $10 a month; installing WordPress on your hosting server can usually be done with a single click; you have unlimited customization options; you can set up your own online shop and sell books directly from your website.

But take it from someone who spent a few years making a living as a WordPress theme designer and developer and who has had multiple self-hosted WordPress sites: this is terrible advice for a lot of authors. Here's the downside of a self-hosted WordPress site that you rarely hear about:

- The security and reliability of pretty much all affordable WordPress-equipped web hosts is terrible. I tried a number of different hosts over the years, and on every single one, not only did my websites sometimes go down because of too much traffic on another website that shared my hosting server, but I've also spent hours trying to salvage websites and clean them up after they got hacked or had malware installed. I finally threw in the towel after my self-hosted author blog was completely wiped out by a hacker.

- Maintenance can be never-ending. You're constantly having to update your theme as well as any plug-ins you're using to extend the functionality of your site. And sometimes a new plug-in update will break your theme, and vice versa. You can spend so much time on back-end site maintenance that you don't have time to work on the actual content—not to mention time to write your next book.

- Customer service tends to be lackluster. Again, I've used a number of hosts, including many of the most highly recommended, and each and every one of them were less than helpful whenever I ran into a real problem.
- Let's face it—if you're a truly broke author, even a cheap host can be difficult to afford.

So what do I recommend instead?

If You Have a Little Money...

I recommend a combination hosting and content management platform like Squarespace, WordPress.com, Webs.com or Weebly, each of which offers different hosting tiers at different price points, with more functionality added on the higher you go. While these tend to cost more than your typical shared-hosting plan (which is what all of the affordable WordPress content management system hosts are, meaning that you share your hosting server with several, if not dozens, of other websites over which you have no control), they are much more secure, not to mention easy to use and hassle-free.

My author website is on WordPress.com. It uses a stripped down version of the WordPress content management system (I told you this could be confusing), but in exchange for losing a lot of options and functionality that I don't actually need, I get a secure, low-maintenance website on my own domain. I chose the personal plan, which is their lowest paid tier at $48 per year. It has everything I need, and my domain was included in the price (note: Wordpress.com recently informed me that they will no longer be including a free domain in their hosting packages, so keep that in mind as you consider your options).

WordPress.com won't let you have any e-commerce functionality on your website at that level, though. If you want to sell books or other products directly from your website, you're better off going with Squarespace or Weebly, each of which offers built-in shops and e-commerce functionality for a not-unreasonable price.

Before you decide, not only should you shop around to compare prices and features, but you should also do some research on what is involved in selling products online in your state. My state's sales tax laws make selling even digital products like e-books directly from my website so much of a hassle that it's not worth it to me to bother (and don't even get me started on trying to keep up with European sales tax), so I don't. You might decide it's not worth it to you, either.

If You Have No Money...

You can create a lovely website for free at WordPress.com, Weebly.com or Wix.com. If you do plan to keep a blog, many indie authors also do quite well using Blogspot blogs as their official websites.

The downside of this is that your free website will probably display ads over which you have no control, and unless you pay a small fee for setting up your domain (often in addition to the cost of domain registration), you'll be stuck with a web address that looks like yourauthorname.yourwebhost.com.

I actually had my author site set up on a free WordPress.com account for a few years before I upgraded to the personal hosting plan. It wasn't ideal, but it was fine. If you're able to afford the eight or nine bucks it costs to register your own .com domain, here's a little work-around I used during that time: set up URL forwarding on your domain host and point it to your free website's address. Once visitors reach your site, they'll still see the third-party domain, but you'll be able to use your own domain in all of your communication, including books and business cards, which will look more official and professional.

While it's ideal to have a paid hosting plan with no ads and your own domain, don't sweat it if that's not in your budget right now. There are plenty of free options that will do just fine to get you started, and a free website is infinitely better than no website.

Your Mailing List

Now we come to the crux of your platform: your mailing list.

To be honest, it took me a long time to fully grasp the importance of having a mailing list, and this might be something you grapple with, too. I was a blogger for a long time before I became an author, and my thinking regarding mailing lists went something like this:

"If I have a blog, what's the point of a mailing list? Can't people just subscribe to my blog? What would I even do with a mailing list? Wouldn't I have to send out a newsletter? Who has time for that? And what would I put in a newsletter that isn't already on my blog? Wouldn't that be redundant and annoying? Who would even sign up for that?"

And so for years, based on my faulty reasoning, I didn't bother with building a mailing list. It wasn't until I started my own freelance business that I finally understood how a mailing list could be useful, but even then, I still struggled with how that usefulness could apply to my writing.

So let's break down all of my objections and look at them one by one.

"If I have a blog, what's the point of a mailing list?"

If someone subscribes to your blog, they're saying they want to be regular readers of your blog. That's it. That doesn't mean they'll actually read everything you post—only that they want the option and to make it easy by having it appear in their feed reader or their inbox. A blog subscription is about the reader's convenience, period. It doesn't give you any special permission to contact them.

When someone signs up to your mailing list, on the other hand, they are handing you their e-mail address with the understanding that you'll use it at some point to tell them something you would like them to know. They are giving you permission to contact them directly, because they want to know about what you have to offer (and if they change their minds, they'll let you know by unsubscribing).

A blog subscriber finds your content interesting enough to casually follow. A mailing list subscriber is so interested in what you're creating that they don't want to miss a thing—and is also far more likely than a casual blog subscriber to click a link to buy your new release when you e-mail them to tell them it's available.

"What would I even do with a mailing list?"

A mailing list gives you the ability and opportunity to e-mail your subscribers and let them know when you have something to offer that they have already expressed interest in by the implication of signing up to your list to begin with. It doesn't mean you have to stay in contact with them constantly. It doesn't mean you must send out a regular newsletter, although that is generally the best practice, so that your subscribers don't go so long from hearing from you that they forget who you are or why they signed up to get e-mail from you. And it doesn't mean you have to, or should, send out pushy, sales-y marketing e-mails. At it's most basic, a mailing list simply provides a way for you to contact your most devoted following and say, "Hey, I made a new thing I think you'll like. Here's where you can get it."

"What would I put in a newsletter that isn't already on my blog?"

Like I said, you don't have to send out a newsletter. The truth is that readers are divided on newsletters. While I don't have scientific data to back that up, based on online discussions I've seen regarding the matter, roughly half of readers and fans enjoy author newsletters, while the other half or so could do without them. Your biggest challenge is to figure out what your ideal reader (more on that in the next chapter) would prefer, and tailor your communication accordingly. If Ideal Reader isn't someone who enjoys newsletters, then skip it, and only e-mail your list when you have actual news—i.e., cover reveals, new releases, sales, author appearances or other special events, etc.

If, on the other hand, Ideal Reader is in the other camp, then write about things that will appeal to her. The key is to make sure your newsletter content is one of two things, and preferably both: useful and/or entertaining.

If you're a non-fiction author, it should be easy to come up with useful information to provide your subscribers. Simply expand on the topic and information covered in your book. For fiction authors, entertaining is a no-brainer: simply do what you do best and include a story in each missive. Some fiction authors include a drabble—a piece of microfiction that's exactly 100 words long—in each issue. Some include longer works of flash fiction. You could also give your readers exclusive sneak previews of your upcoming books or your current work in progress.

In either case, it's also not a bad idea to include a little bit about yourself—just don't go overboard and treat your newsletter like a Livejournal post. A paragraph or two that gives your readers a behind-the-scenes look at your life and writing process tends to go over well.

Here's the template I use for my monthly fiction author newsletter. Feel free to adapt it for your own use.

- A short recap of what's been going on in my life and what I've been working on since the last letter
- A quick rundown of what I have coming up in the future
- A section mentioning any current sales or promotions, and any other relevant news
- A section with links to my latest blog posts
- A section talking about what I've been reading and/or watching
- Finally, after the sign-off, I include something fun to read: an exclusive, never-before-seen flash fic, a new chapter of my upcoming novel, or a deleted scene from an already-released novel.

If you'd like to see my template in action, go to http://bit.ly/JMB-Archive.

"Who has time for that?"

This is actually a valid question. As with a blog, if you don't have time to send out a newsletter on a consistent schedule, then feel free to skip it and stick to timely announcements.

In fact, as of this writing, I'm getting ready to scale back my own newsletter from going out monthly to once every other month. I've reached a point where my plate is overloaded with writing projects and having to make time to write a monthly newsletter is causing more stress than it's worth. Also, I think my readers would rather have me working on my next release than adding to their monthly inbox clutter.

Now that we've covered the why of your mailing list, let's get into the how.

Your Mailing List Service Provider

Once upon a time, you could simply create a group folder in your e-mail contacts and fire off an e-mail directly from your e-mail client. But those days are long gone, so don't even think about trying that. It will only get your e-mails dumped in spam folders across the globe and get your e-mail address blacklisted.

Fortunately, today there are a number of mailing list service providers that go way beyond simply managing contacts and composing and sending e-mails, most notably AWeber, Constant Contact and Mailchimp, among others. These services not only provide sign-up forms and other tools to help build your list, they also provide templates that make it easy to create e-mail campaigns that are attractive and easy to read. And more importantly, they let you create auto-responders—we'll talk about why that's important in a bit.

For the broke author, your best bet is to sign up with Mailchimp.com. This service will provide everything you need to build and manage your list, create and manage campaigns, and track the performance of each e-mail you send. Better yet, it's free as long as you have fewer than 2,000 subscribers (and by the time you breach that barrier, chances are you'll no longer be a broke author).

Getting Subscribers Onto Your List

Here's the bad news—getting subscribers is the hard part. But there are ways to make it easier. Here are some do's and don'ts that will help make it happen:

DO put your sign-up form (or a link to the form hosted on Mailchimp, if you're unable to embed a form on your website) everywhere on your website that makes sense: your homepage, a separate landing page just for sign-ups, your blog/news page sidebar, the bottom of every book page, the footer of every post. Make it ridiculously easy for your visitors to sign up.

DO use a pop-up form on your site inviting people to sign up. Yes, pop-ups are annoying. Yes, everybody hates them. And yet? For some reason, they actually work. So get over your qualms and use them.

DON'T rely on your newsletter, or the promise of being the first to know about a new release, or on your sparkling personality or clever wit to entice people to sign-up.

DO create a subscriber magnet and offer it as an incentive for signing up. A subscriber magnet is a free gift that you will give to every new subscriber. If you write non-fiction, this might be something useful to your audience like a checklist, a mini-course, a set of downloadable worksheets that can be used with your book… the possibilities might not be endless, but there are a lot of them.

If you write fiction, you could offer an exclusive short story or novella set in the same universe as your book or series. If you're writing a series, you might even consider giving away the first or second book in your series. If you've only got one book, or you're still working on your first book, offer an extended preview.

Yes, reader magnets sometimes take time to put together. But they're the most effective tool for growing your list, so don't skip this step. For more information and ideas on how to employ this tactic effectively, check out Reader Magnets, a free e-book from bestselling self-published thriller author Nick Stephenson. Head to daydreamerpublishing.wordpress.com/brokeauthor/resources to find the link.

DON'T say on your sign-up call to action, "Sign up for my mailing list" or "Sign up for news about new releases and special offers!"

DO say "I have this gift, here's why I think you'll like it, it's yours if you enter your e-mail below and let me know where to send it."

DON'T sell, trade or share your list with anyone for any reason. Not only is it illegal, it's also an unethical violation of your subscriber's trust.

DON'T buy other people's e-mail lists. This is also illegal, and sending mass e-mails to people who didn't specifically opt in to receive them will get you flagged as a spammer.

DO place a link to your sign-up form on all of your social media profiles. If you have multiple links to promote—say, a link to buy your book and/or a link to your latest blog post—use a free service like Linktree (http://linktr.ee) to manage them and keep the link to your mailing list at the top.

DO include sign-up links and an ad for your subscriber magnet in your books (more on this in the next section).

DON'T fret over your tiny list. These things take time.

DO treat your small number of subscribers like gold. If you only have five subscribers, show up for those five people the same as you would if you had five hundred or five thousand. Those five people are your most devoted fans. Treat them like VIPs.

Your All-Important Auto-Responder Campaign

When someone signs up to your mailing list, they should immediately receive a short welcome e-mail thanking them for trusting you with their e-mail, and providing a link to where they can download their free gift. You can set this up as an auto-responder—a pre-written e-mail that automatically gets sent when an action, such as opting in to your list, is performed.

This is the bare minimum of how you can and should use auto-responders to interact with new subscribers. Savvy authors will set up a series of auto-responders, set to trickle out every few days after someone signs up, to tell the subscriber a little more about themselves, as well as their books and any other products or services they have to offer. Again, you don't want to do this in a pushy, sales-y way, but simply, "I hope you're enjoying your free gift. If so, then you might also like these books I wrote," and then let the reader know where to find them.

Will this cause some subscribers to turn right around and unsubscribe? A few, undoubtedly. But that's okay. More likely than not, those are people who only signed up to snag the freebie and had no intention of staying subscribed. That does happen sometimes, and it sucks when it does, but don't let it bother you. Look at your auto-responder campaign as a filter that weeds out the freebie-hunters from the true fans. It's no use inflating your subscriber count with the addresses of people who will never even bother to open your e-mails—especially considering you're only allowed a limited number of subscribers on the free plan. You want every e-mail address on your list to count, to represent a genuine fan of your work.

For this reason, I see it as a good thing whenever I lose a subscriber—they weren't really a fan anyway, and they made room for someone else who genuinely cares about what I can offer them. And your genuine fans will appreciate the extra e-mails letting them know what they might have missed. In any case, you'll retain a lot more subscribers than you'll lose with this method.

For a more in-depth look at how to grow your list and use

auto-responders to sell more books, sign up for Tim Grahl's free training course at Booklaunch.com.

Back to Your Books: Pulling it All Together

The final stone to lay in your platform's foundation brings us back to your books—specifically, the back matter. In the back of every book you publish, be sure to include the following three things:

1. Your author bio. Use the shorter version of your bio, and include a link (in your paperback, simply include the URL) to your website and an invitation to visit and sign up for your mailing list.
2. A letter from the author—not to be confused with an author's note that discusses some aspect of writing the book. This letter is best placed immediately after the end of the story, where the reader will see it while they're still emotionally or intellectually engaged with your book, and it should say something along these lines:

Dear Reader,

Thank you for taking the time to read my book. I hope you enjoyed it. If so, I would appreciate it if you would swipe left to rate the book and leave a review. I also hope you'll stop by my website [link] and sign up so you'll be sure not to miss my next book. I'll send you a free gift just for signing up.

Love,
Your name

3. An ad letting readers know about your subscriber magnet and how to get it. It doesn't have to be a graphic ad, but those tend to be more attention-getting. This is another thing for which Canva.com can come in handy—just remember to insert the high-resolution print-quality PDF version in your paperback. Place this ad both in the front and the back of the book—that way it will also be visible in your book sample, and your reader will also get a final reminder before closing your book.

Once you have more than one book to your name, you'll also want to return to your first book and include an "Also by" page that lets readers know about other books you've written. The beauty of self-publishing is that you can keep coming back and updating this page as you add more books to your back catalog so that it always stays up-to-date.

Congratulations! If you've followed these steps, you've not only built a solid author platform on which to grow your writing and publishing career—you've also created an automated marketing machine that will keep working for you to build your following and sell your books while you're busy building up your catalog with new books.

As both your back catalog and your following grow, you'll want to add in other forms of marketing and outreach. We'll look at some of those, as well as best practices, in the next chapter. But for now, you've got a great foundation for success, and the best thing you can do is focus on expanding that foundation by writing your next book.

87

Let's Go Fishing

If you've studied the principles of online marketing at all, then you're probably already familiar with the concept of the sales funnel. But in case you're not, here's the gist of it:

Everything you do online should funnel the consumer toward a specific goal or call to action.

The wide mouth of your funnel is all of your outreach — your social media, your website and/or blog, the ads in the back of your books, guest posts, interviews, etc. The goal of all of these is to drive readers to perform a specific action.

You might think that action is to buy your books. You're about half right. While that's the ultimate outcome you're hoping for, your actual, more concrete goal is to get them to sign up to your mailing list, which is the most powerful tool you have for connecting with your readers and selling more books.

While the funnel metaphor is helpful, I prefer a fishing metaphor. Your mailing list is the boat. Your readers are the fish. Your subscriber magnet is the bait. The rest of your platform is your rod, reel and tackle — everything you do to entice readers, hook them and pull them into your boat. And book sales are the delicious fish fry you get to enjoy as the result of all your hard work.

But you can't enjoy that fish fry (mmm, hush puppies) unless you first reel the fish into the boat.

In this chapter, we'll explore some of the elements that make up your rod and reel. But first, you need to know who, precisely, you're fishing for.

Know Your Ideal Reader

In business marketing, there exists the concept of the ideal client. A business will define a type of persona, or multiple personas, who have a use, need or desire for the product or service that the business is selling, and target all of their marketing at people who match those personas.

In book marketing, that concept translates to the ideal reader. This is the person, or persons, who will have a strong need or desire to read your book, who will go beyond just buying and reading to becoming a true fan who will evangelize your work and be likely to read everything you publish — or at least every book in the series that hooked them.

I'm sure you can imagine how identifying your ideal reader — the big fish you want to catch — can be useful. Once you know who this person is, you will tailor all of your marketing and outreach — which networks you focus your attention on, the content you post and share, how you brand yourself, etc. — to that particular reader, who represents the type of reader and book buyer you most want to reach.

So how do you figure out who your ideal reader is?

Someone You Already Know

It could be that you've already got an ideal reader in mind. If there is someone you always imagine reading your books as you write them, who loves your writing (and not just because they happen to love you) and can't wait for you to finish your next project, who tends to be a fan of the genre in which you're writing and is happy to spend money to support your work, then this person is a perfect model on which to base your ideal reader.

Someone You Imagine

Because your ideal reader is more or less a fictional persona, you can feel free to make them up whole cloth. Starting with the typical fan of your genre, imagine the type of person most likely to fall in love with your book, and create a character sketch of this person to serve as your Ideal Reader Profile.

You

I write the kind of fiction I love to read. So when I first tried to imagine my ideal reader, logic dictated that she would be someone very much like myself. If you're a fan of your own work, or of that type of work, you can absolutely base your ideal reader persona on yourself.

A Compilation of Existing Readers

If this isn't your first book, or if you've already got an established platform or following, then you have access to data that you can mine to craft an Ideal Reader Profile. If this is your first book and you're starting from scratch, then you can start with one (or a combination) of the above methods, and then use this method to tweak your persona as you gain a following. Here are a few ways to gather information on the people most likely to fall into your Ideal Reader category:

- Ask your mailing list. Even a tiny list can be helpful. When I first did this, I sent a reader poll out to my relatively small mailing list. Only five people responded and took the poll, but those five people represented my most hard-core fans. The information they provided me was invaluable in helping me craft my Ideal Reader profile.
- Study your reviewers. On Amazon and Goodreads, pay attention to what reviewers say they like about your books. Click on the profiles of people who've left you glowing reviews. Reviewers don't always fill out their profiles, but when they do, those profiles tend to be filled with valuable information about who you should focus on targeting.
- Pay attention to who is engaging with your social media posts. The followers that engage the most enthusiastically with posts about your books or writing might simply be fellow writers trying to be supportive — or they might be readers who are enthusiastic about your work. The latter could be a big clue as to what your ideal reader is like.

Whichever method, or combination of methods, you use, take this step seriously and don't shortchange it. Take your time developing a persona, or even multiple personas, that define your ideal reader, filling in as many details about their lives and personalities as possible. And remember that this is the person most likely to love your work, not simply be a fan of your genre, although that's a good place to start. Just don't rely on stereotypes or assumptions to fill in the blanks. For example, you might be writing a young adult novel, but keep in mind that some of the biggest fans of YA — and the ones with the most money to spend

— are grown adults with kids of their own.

Here are some of the most important factors in identifying your ideal reader you'll need to know:

- What is their age, gender, occupation and family makeup? If your ideal reader is a fifteen-year-old female student, your marketing and branding will be quite different than if it's aimed at a forty-year-old stay-at-home mom or a 50 year old corporate VP who's thinking about retirement.
- Where do they prefer to hang out online? This is crucial, because it will determine where you hang out online.
- What is their biggest pain point? Is there a specific problem they're struggling with that your nonfiction book will provide answers to? Are they hungry for an escape that your novel will provide? Are they fed up with formulaic genre fiction and you can offer them something refreshingly original? Knowing their problem, and how your book can help solve it, is the juiciest bait for your hook.
- What are they into? What TV shows or movies do they love? What are their favorite books (besides yours)? Do they have pets? Are they dog people or cat people? Do they cook or eat out? Are they foodies or health nuts? Do they prefer coffee or tea?

This might seem like frivolous information, but these details are where you will connect with your ideal reader on a personal level, where they will learn to see you as a person and not simply a book writing automaton. But be authentic. Don't pander to your ideal reader's likes, but look for common ground where you can make a connection with them.

Are there shows your reader loves that you also love? Do you adore any of the same books or authors? Do you enjoy any of the same hobbies? Once you find your common ground, use that as a focal point to guide your content — your blog posts, social media posts, tweets, retweets, etc. This is not just how you will connect with potential readers — this is how you will build your tribe.

Content Marketing

Also known as inbound marketing or pull marketing, content marketing is the rod and reel you will use to pull your ideal reader fish into your boat.

What does content marketing mean? It simply means tailoring your online content to your ideal reader's interests in order to pull them in and entice them to sign up to your mailing list. This encompasses everything you do online as an author: what you blog about, what you tweet about, what content from other people that you choose to share, the content that makes up your subscriber magnet, your Facebook and Instagram posts, YouTube videos, Pinterest pins… all of it.

Content Marketing and the Sales Funnel

Here's how content marketing works as part of your sales funnel, or rather, your fishing boat:

1. You bait your hook by tailoring your social media posts to your ideal readers, posting content you know they'll be likely to enjoy and engage with, in order to connect with those who fit your ideal reader profile and build up your following.
2. You write an evergreen post on your blog—or on a platform like Medium, if you've decided against having a blog—that will appeal to your ideal reader by addressing their pain

point. An evergreen post is one that isn't time sensitive and will remain relevant months or years in the future. Seed your post with key search words that will bring in potential ideal readers from search engines. Include a link and an invitation to download your free subscriber magnet in the footer of the post.

3. Broadcast a link to your post on your social media. Use relevant hashtags so that the link will be seen not just by your followers, but by other people interested in that type of content.

4. Ideally, a decent number of people will see the link, click through to your post, like your content enough to share it with their networks, and also sign up to your mailing list while they're there, becoming a willing member of your tribe and giving you permission to let them know about your books.

5. Go back to number one and repeat the process, over and over again.

Content Marketing Tools and Guidelines

You can get the most out of your content by utilizing a few of these tricks:

- Use hashtags. As mentioned above, using the right hashtags on Twitter and Instagram can vastly expand your reach, which is especially helpful if you don't have a large following. It's helpful to know which hashtags your ideal reader is most likely to follow, but they also need to be relevant to your content. Use a free tool like Hashtagify.me to find popular relevant hashtags to attach to your posts or tweets.

- Use SEO keywords in your articles and posts. SEO stands for "search engine optimization." Using relevant keywords or phrases that your ideal reader might search on to find content like yours can pull in readers from Google and other search engines. You can use KeywordTool.io to help you determine the best keywords to use throughout your content. Just don't go overboard. The best practice regarding this is to use one or two keywords or phrases no more than two to four times each. Any more than that could get your post penalized for keyword stuffing.

- Use repetition. The "rule of seven" is a well-known marketing principle that says someone needs to be exposed to your message at least seven times before they decide to take action. So don't be afraid to repeat yourself and repost links—just don't be obnoxious about it by repeating the exact same tweets or posts several times in a row. If you have a blog, Missinglettr.com is a great free tool for creating drip campaigns that will automatically "drip" social media posts linking back to your blog and spread them out over an entire year.

- Schedule your marketing posts. While it's not a great idea to rely entire on scheduled and automated content for your social media—it's way more effective if you sign on from time to time and spend time personally interacting and engaging with your followers—you can use an app like Buffer.com or Tweetdeck.twitter.com to schedule your marketing content to post to your social media. This is not only a time saver, it's also a great way to make sure your promotional content is evenly spread out among your more personal and fun content so that your feed won't come across as spammy.

You're probably starting to get the picture that content marketing works best if you have your own blog, and I can't deny that this is true. A blog is going to give you the best opportunity to post evergreen content that you can keep utilizing to pull readers to your website.

But that doesn't mean you can't make it work without a blog. Content marketing isn't limited to your own platform—you can also make use of other people's platforms via interviews, guest posts and getting your books reviewed on book blogs, all of which can point back to your website and, more importantly, your mailing list.

You can also post articles on platforms like Medium and LinkedIn that can include calls to action inviting readers to visit your website and download your free subscriber magnet. And if you prefer talking to writing blog posts, you can utilize YouTube, Instagram Stories or Snapchat to create a video blog, or "vlog," that can serve as part of your platform and help funnel people toward your list. The best path will depend largely on your ideal reader's preference, as well as on your own.

Content marketing is without a doubt the most effective way you can reach new readers and pull them in to your mailing list boat, without spending money on pricey ads. And if you hate sales and marketing as much as many introverted writers, myself included, do, then you'll find content marketing to be a Godsend, because it doesn't involve pushy sales tactics. It's simply doing what you do best: writing and creating engaging content, and sharing it with the people who will most want to read it.

Social Media

Social media can be a powerful tool for hooking and reeling in your big fish, a.k.a. your ideal reader. But if you don't approach it the right way, it can be a useless waste of your valuable time. Even worse, too much time on social media can be an emotionally draining black hole that sucks up both your time and your energy, leaving you with nothing left to give to your writing.

There's not enough space in this book for a comprehensive guide to using social media, but here's a helpful list of what to do — and what NOT to do — to improve the usefulness of your social networks, as well as your overall experience.

Dos and Don'ts of Social Media

DO protect yourself. Feel free to mute, unfollow and filter out any people or content that detract from your experience.

DO feel free to block anyone who puts out a creeper vibe. On social media, it pays to trust your gut.

DON'T feel obligated to follow back everyone who follows you. Therein lies madness.

DO check out the profiles of those who follow you and only follow them back if you're generally interested in what they're posting or tweeting.

DO block robots and spammers. Not only are they irritating, but they'll artificially inflate your follower count — and that's a bad thing.

DON'T follow just to get followers, and ESPECIALLY DON'T turn right around and unfollow those who follow you. You don't want to go to the special hell.

DO grow your following organically, filling your network with actual people who are genuinely interested in what you have to offer. A large follower count is meaningless if your followers are robots, pushy marketers, and people who never bother to read your posts.

DON'T spam your feed with a constant bombardment of self-promotion. A good rule of thumb is the 20/80 rule — 20 percent self-promotion and 80 percent other types of content.

DO retweet and share other people's content generously (just don't forget to tailor what you share to your ideal reader's interests)

DO post about yourself — your thoughts and opinions, your hobbies, what you're watching, listening to or reading, what's happening in your day, your writing process, etc.

DON'T post divisive political opinions, unless you're a political writer and/or you don't care if you offend and turn off roughly half of your potential readership.

DO feel free to use some automation and cross-posting — i.e., auto-tweeting a new blog post when it publishes, pushing your Instagram posts to Twitter and/or Facebook, tweeting your Goodreads reviews or Pinterest pins, scheduling updates, shares and promotional posts. Just don't rely too heavily on this. Think of it as a way to fill in when you're unable to engage in person.

DO tailor your content to each individual network as much as possible.

DO engage with your followers and the people you follow. Respond to comments, mentions and retweets, and engage in conversations with the people in your network and in the hashtags you follow.

DO use eye-catching images. Feel free to post photos (especially of your pets) and use Canva or Adobe Spark to create sharable graphics.

DO repeat your promotional links — just spread out the repeats among fresher content so you won't come across as spammy. And make sure the repeat posts aren't completely identical, which is against Twitter's TOS.

DON'T EVER spam someone's direct messages or private inbox with links to buy your book or follow you on another network. Don't send anyone a private message about anything unless and until you've already engaged with that person and established some type of acquaintance or relationship. To do otherwise is pure spam, not to mention invasive and rude.

DON'T look at social media as an effective way to directly market and sell your books. It's not.

DO view social media as an effective way to network with

professionals in your field and indirectly market your books by making authentic connections with potential ideal readers and growing your tribe.

DON'T try to do it all or be everywhere.

DO focus your efforts on the networks where your ideal reader is most likely to be. And DO only focus on one or two networks at a time until you learn how to use them effectively.

DON'T feel obligated to stick with something if you feel like it's a waste of your time and energy.

DO have fun — and if it reaches a point where it's no longer fun, do feel free to take as long of a break as you need.

Advertising, Outreach and Reviews

Everything I've discussed up to now is basically free, although it will cost you time. But that's how it goes when you're a broke author. I'm not going to go over the more expensive marketing options here, because that wouldn't really fit the thesis of this book.

Instead, I'm going to reassure you that it's okay if you don't have an advertising budget. The fact is that, while paid advertising can be a highly effective investment if you have an established back catalog that will also enjoy a spike in sales subsequent to reaching and gaining new fans, if you've only got one or two books to your name, paid advertising generally has a terrible return on investment.

Influencer Outreach

This early in your career, apart from content marketing and building your mailing list, the most effective way to get exposure for your books is to reach out to reviewers, book bloggers and other influencers who read and write or talk about books in your genre. Be sure to read and follow their guidelines carefully, and be aware that you'll need to provide them with a free reviewer copy of your book. Some reviewers only accept physical copies, so you might have to do some digging to find those who will accept e-books, which won't cost you anything to provide.

Think beyond book blogs, too. Don't be afraid to reach out to podcasters and vloggers who might be open to discussing your book. And while reviews can be a tough sell because it requires a big chunk of the influencer's time, they might be more open to granting you an interview or letting you write a guest post, which will save them time by providing them with free content for their own audience.

Just be respectful when reaching out to influencers. Don't spam their private messages, and if they post guidelines for how to reach out to them, follow them. Focus on what you can do for them, not on what they can do for you. It's also not a bad idea to follow them on social media and establish an acquaintance to warm them up to you before contacting them directly. Cold e-mails can work, but warm e-mails tend to get better results.

While these methods can be effective for gaining spikes in sales and, more importantly, growing your reader base, again, the more books you have in your catalog, the more effective they'll be. So don't get bogged down in promoting your first book. For now, set up your platform and automated marketing machine as outlined in the last chapter, and save the more advanced tactics for when you've got a few books to offer new readers.

Your Strategy

Take time to answer the questions at the end of each chapter to help you develop your budget publishing strategy.

1. What are my longterm goals as an author? Take a few minutes to think this out and write them down.

2. What are my values? What is most important to me in life? What do I most want to be spending my time on?

3. How can self-publishing help me prioritize those values in my life?

4. Write three words that describe my author brand (you can write more than three, but try to narrow it down to the best three).

5. Which genre best describes my book?

6. How much can I afford to budget for an author website?

7. How important is it to be able to sell books directly on my website?

8. Based on this information, which web site platform(s) do I think might best serve my goals?

9. Which strategy or strategies will I use to define my ideal reader?

10. Write down everything you already know about your ideal reader.

11. Based on this information, where online will my time and effort best be spent to help me build my book tribe?

12. Use this space to brainstorm ideas for how you will reach out to your ideal reader and reel them into your boat.

13. Use this space to brainstorm ideas for reader magnets.

14. Use this space to brainstorm ideas for what to include in your mailing list.

A Final Word

Do the best you can with what you have, right where you are. I don't know who first came up with that bit of wisdom, but it's a guiding principle in my life, and it applies to self-publishing as much as it does to anything else.

It's so easy to get hung up on waiting for the ideal circumstances to step out and go after our dreams. But I'm here to tell you that ideal circumstances don't exist. Whatever you've been told you have to have before you can publish your book, however much you've been told that it costs to produce a book that has any chance to succeed, I want you to know that you already have everything you need to start.

More importantly, I want to reassure you that when it comes to self-publishing, there is no expiration date on improving, promoting or selling your book. Each book you bring into the world has an endless shelf life, and you can come back and improve it and relaunch it as often as you like until you get the results you want.

So stop waiting. Use what you have. Do the best you can. And start right where you are.

Now go forth and publish your book, and do it again and again until you're no longer a broke author.

IV

Resources

Helpful Links

The self-publishing landscape is constantly changing, and new tools and resources are being developed all the time. While this section includes all of the links from this book in one handy place, I keep a more dynamic list of helpful links at daydreamerpublishing. wordpress.com/brokeauthor/resources.

Editing and Proofreading

ProWritingAid -
  https://prowritingaid.com/
Fiverr -
  http://fiverr.com
Grammarly -
  https//www.grammarly.com/

Formatting and Book Design

Scrivener -
  https://www.literatureandlatte.com/
  scrivener/overview
Vellum -
  https://vellum.pub/
Calibre -

https://calibre-ebook.com

How to Format Ebooks with Many Pictures in Calibre - http://selfpublishingadvice.org/production-how-to-format-ebooks-with-many-pictures-in-calibre/

Open Office Writer - https://www.openoffice.org/product/writer.html

Smashwords - https://www.smashwords.com

Smashwords Style Guide - https://www.smashwords.com/books/view/52

Draft2Digital - https://www.draft2digital.com

Reedsy Book Editor - https://reedsy.com/write-a-book

Download a free MS Word template from Kindle Direct Publishing - https://kdp.amazon.com/en_US/help/topic/G201834230

Cover Design

The Book Designer - https://www.thebookdesigner.com/

Cover Designers on Fiverr - https://daydreamerpublishing.wordpress.com/broke-author/resources/#Fiverr_short_list

Canva - https://www.canva.com/

Gimp - https://www.gimp.org/

Gimp + Canva Tutorial - https://daydreamerpublishing.wordpress.com/2018/10/13/

how-canva-gimp-can-produce-a-stunning-cover-for-your-
paperback/

Publishing Platforms

The Creative Penn explains Amazon key words -
   https://www.thecreativepenn.com/
   book-categories-keywords/
Kindle Direct Publishing -
   https://kdp.amazon.com
Draft2Digital -
   https://www.draft2digital.com
Smashwords -
   https://smashwords.com
IngramSpark -
   https://ingramspark.com
ACX -
   https://www.acx.com/help/authors/200484540
Findaway Voices -
   https://findawayvoices.com/
Audacity -
   https://sourceforge.net/projects/audacity/

Platform and Author Brand

The Book Designer - How to Build Your Author Brand from
Scratch (Blog Post) -
   https://www.thebookdesigner.com/2015/12/
   how-to-build-your-author-brand-from-scratch-
   and-why-you-need-to/
The Creative Penn - 7 Best Ways To Build An Authentic Author

Brand (Blog Post) -
   https://www.thecreativepenn.com/2017/11/10/
   authentic-author-brand/
Kobo Writing Life - The Essential of Book Cover Design (Blog
Post) -
   https://kobowritinglife.com/2016/07/27/
   the-essentials-of-book-cover-design/

Your Website

Wordpress.com - https://wordpress.com/
Squarespace - https://www.squarespace.com/
Webs - webs.com
Wix - https://www.wix.com/
Weebly - https://www.weebly.com/
Blogger - https://www.blogger.com
Internetbs.net - https://internetbs.net/

Your Mailing List

My newsletter archive -
   http://bit.ly/JMBNewsletter
Mailchimp -
   https://mailchimp.com/
Reader Magnets -
   https://www.blog.yourfirst10kreaders.com/
   what-are-reader-magnets/
Linktree -
   https://linktr.ee/

Content Marketing Tools

Hashtagify - https://hashtagify.me/
Keyword Tool - https://keywordtool.io/
Missinglettr - https://missinglettr.com
Buffer - https://buffer.com/
Tweetdeck - https://tweetdeck.twitter.com/

Free Photo & Image Libraries

DISCLAIMER: These sites all contain free, copyright-free images that are either released under a Creative Commons license or are public domain. As far as I know, they are all free for commercial use and don't require attribution, but you should always double check the license on any photo you want to use to be sure.

Unsplash - https://unsplash.com/
Pixabay - https://pixabay.com/
Pexels - https://www.pexels.com/
Picography - https://picography.co
Freestocks.org - https://freestocks.org/
Gratisography - https://gratisography.com/
Picjumbo - https://picjumbo.com/
Kaboompics - https://kaboompics.com
Lifeofpix - https://www.lifeofpix.com/
NewOldStock (Vintage stock images in the public domain)-
    https://nos.twnsnd.co/
Wikimedia Commons -
    https://commons.wikimedia.org/wiki/
    Category:Images

If that's not enough, you can also use the advance search settings on Flickr.com to search for photos licensed under Creative Commons, and click the Tools button on Google Image Search to search under Usage Rights for images that are labeled for reuse.

Keep Learning

While reading this book is a great start, learning all there is to know about self-publishing and how to do it well is an ongoing endeavor. To expand your knowledge base, I recommend acquainting yourself with the following resources:

Books

Your First 1,000 Copies by Tim Grahl
How to Market a Book by Joanna Penn
Newsletter Ninja by Tammi Labrecque
Let's Get Digital and *Strangers to Superfans* by David Gaughran

Blogs

The Publishing School Blog -
   http://daydreamerpublishing.wordpress.com/blog
The Creative Penn -
   http://thecreativepenn.com
The Book Designer -
   http://thebookdesigner.com
David Gaughran -
   http://davidgaughran.com
Dean Wesley Smith -

http://deanwesleysmith.com
Kristine Kathryn Rusch -
  http://kriswrites.com

Podcasts

The Creative Penn
Self Publishing Show
Kobo Writing Life
AskAlli: Self-Publishing Advice Podcast
Happy Self-Publishing Show
Dabblers vs. Doers
Smart Author with Mark Coker

Free Courses

My free editing course at Daydreamer Publishing -
  https://daydreamerpublishing.wordpress.com/
  free-editing-course/
Tim Grahl's free e-mail training course at Booklaunch.com -
  https://booklaunch.com/start-here/
Nick Stephenson's First 10,000 Readers Course -
  https://www.yourfirst10kreaders.com/

The Broke Author Newsletter

The Broke Author Newsletter will deliver the latest self-publishing news straight to your inbox! You'll also get free goodies, exclusive tools and resources, and sneak peeks as upcoming books in the Broke Author series.

Head to daydreamerpublishing.wordpress.com/brokeauthor to tell us where to send it!

Thanks for Reading!

Hi!

Thanks for reading Self-Publishing for the Broke Author. I really hope you enjoyed it, or at least found it helpful. Either way, please consider leaving a review! Good or bad, your review will help other folks find this book and decide whether it's right for them.

If you did enjoy it, you can find more self-publishing info from yours truly at daydreamerpublishing.wordpress.com/blog, where I share tips, news and insights gained from personal experience. While there, you can sign up to the Broke Author newsletter for even more up-to-date self-publishing news, as well as free goodies and sneak previews at upcoming books in the Broke Author series.

Thanks again for reading. I don't take it lightly that you gave this book your time and money, and I hope you feel that both were well spent.

Sincerely,
Jean Bauhaus

Acknowledgements

Much thanks are due to John Davis, Audrey J. Martin, Caitlyn Huehn and Cindy Martens, my very helpful team of beta readers. This is my first non-fiction book and I was very nervous when I sent it to them, and very relieved when they each assured me I was on the right track and that I actually know what I'm talking about.

Thanks also to all of the professionals mentioned throughout this book, in particular Joanna Penn, David Gaughran, Dean Wesley Smith and Kristine Katheryn Rusch. They don't know it (nor do they know me), but they've each served as mentors and inspiration over the years, and neither this book nor my self-publishing career would exist or be where it is without their generous guidance.

Finally, major thanks and appreciation are due to Matt Bauhaus, who not only serves as my editor-in-residence but also does most of the heavy lifting around the house while I'm busy tapping away at my keyboard — not to mention all of the emotional support he provides when I'm certain everything sucks and is doomed to failure, as we writers so often do. I couldn't do any of this without him.

And a very special thank you to Pete, who is the best little writing buddy and lap warmer that there ever was.

About the Author

Jean Bauhaus is a total nerd for good storytelling. She is also incapable of being quiet when someone asks a question she knows the answer to, a trait that is largely responsible for the creation of this book. She grew up in Oklahoma and is a recent transplant to the Ozark mountains, where she lives in the middle of the woods with her husband, Matt, a cat, two box turtles, and a Chihuahua who seems to think he's an actual child. He might have had some encouragement in thinking along those lines.

Jean writes paranormal romance, urban fantasy and horror under the name Jean Marie Bauhaus. You can learn more about her fiction writing at JeanMarieBauhaus.com. She also blogs about and teaches writing and self-publishing at Daydreamer Publishing. She goes by @jmbauhaus on both Twitter and Instagram and would be thrilled if you would say hi to her at either of those places.

Books by Jean Bauhaus

Writing as Jean Marie Bauhaus:

Novels and Novellas

Dominion of the Damned

The Restless Spirits Series:
Restless Spirits
Love Letter: A Restless Spirits Novella
Kindred Spirits
Bound Spirits

Novelettes & Shorts

Shiny: A Clockwork Fairytale
Weather Witch

Collections

Midnight Snacks
Fragments & Fancies: Ficlets, Flach Fiction & Shorts
Women's Work

Find all of Jean's books at JeanMarieBauhaus.com!